THE
LONG-DISTANCE
LEADER

SECOND EDITION

THE LONG-DISTANCE LEADER

SECOND EDITION

Revised Rules for Remarkable Remote and Hybrid Leadership

KEVIN EIKENBERRY
and **WAYNE TURMEL**

BK®

Berrett–Koehler Publishers, Inc.

Berrett-Koehler Publishers, Inc.
1333 Broadway, Suite P100
Oakland, CA 94612-1921
Tel: (510) 817-2277
Fax: (510) 817-2278
bkconnection.com

ORDERING INFORMATION
Quantity sales. Special discounts are available on quantity purchases by corporations, associations, and others. For details, please go to bkconnection.com to see our bulk discounts or contact bookorders@bkpub.com for more information.
Individual sales. Berrett-Koehler publications are available through most bookstores. They can also be ordered directly from Berrett-Koehler: Tel: (800) 929-2929; Fax: (802) 864-7626; bkconnection.com.
Orders for college textbook/course adoption use. Please contact Berrett-Koehler:
Tel: (800) 929-2929; Fax: (802) 864-7626.

Distributed to the US trade and internationally by Penguin Random House Publisher Services.

Berrett-Koehler and the BK logo are registered trademarks of Berrett-Koehler Publishers, Inc.

Printed in Canada

Berrett-Koehler books are printed on long-lasting acid-free paper. When it is available, we choose paper that has been manufactured by environmentally responsible processes. These may include using trees grown in sustainable forests, incorporating recycled paper, minimizing chlorine in bleaching, or recycling the energy produced at the paper mill.

Library of Congress Cataloging-in-Publication Data
Names: Eikenberry, Kevin, 1962- author. | Turmel, Wayne, author.
Title: The long-distance leader : revised rules for remarkable remote and hybrid leadership / Kevin Eikenberry, Wayne Turmel.
Description: Second edition. | Oakland, CA : Berrett-Koehler Publishers, Inc., [2024] | Series: The long-distance worklife series | Includes bibliographical references and index.
Identifiers: LCCN 2024007134 (print) | LCCN 2024007135 (ebook) | ISBN 9798890570222 (paperback) | ISBN 9798890570239 (pdf) | ISBN 9798890570246 (epub)
Subjects: LCSH: Leadership.
Classification: LCC HD57.7 .E384 2024 (print) | LCC HD57.7 (ebook) | DDC 658.4/092— dc23/eng/20240425
LC record available at https://lccn.loc.gov/2024007134
LC ebook record available at https://lccn.loc.gov/2024007135

Second Edition
32 31 30 29 28 27 26 25 24   10 9 8 7 6 5 4 3 2 1

Book producer and text designer: Happenstance Type-O-Rama
Cover designer: Adrian Morgan

This book is dedicated to our teammates at The Kevin Eikenberry Group for—even after all these years—being our inspiration, our support, and occasionally our test kitchen.

Contents

Contents

Rules for Remarkable Remote Leadership

Rule 1   Think about leadership first, location second.

Rule 2   Accept the fact that leading remotely requires you to lead differently and keep learning.

Rule 3   Know that working remotely changes the interpersonal dynamics, even if you don't want it to.

Rule 4   Use technology as a tool, not as a barrier or an excuse.

Rule 5   Leading requires a focus on outcomes, others, and ourselves.

Rule 6   Leading successfully requires achieving goals of many types.

Rule 7   Focus on achieving goals, not just setting them.

Rule 8   Coach your team effectively regardless of where and how they work.

Rule 9   Leading remotely requires more awareness and intention.

Rule 10   If you have one remote team member, you have a Long-Distance Team.

Rule 11   Building trust at a distance doesn't happen by accident.

Rule 12   Identify the leadership results you need, then select the communication tool to achieve them.

Rule 13   Maximize a tool's capabilities or you'll minimize your effectiveness.

Rule 14   Seek feedback to best serve outcomes, others, and ourselves.

Rule 15   Examine your beliefs and self-talk—they define how you lead.

Rule 16   Setting clear boundaries is necessary for you to be an effective Long-Distance Leader.

Rule 17   Balance your priorities to be a Remarkable Long-Distance Leader.

Rule 18   Ensure your leadership development prepares Long-Distance Leaders.

Rule 19   When all else fails, remember Rule 1.

Introduction to the Second Edition

We must adjust to changing times and still hold true to unchanging principles.
—Jimmy Carter, 39th US President

The first edition of this book was conceived in a pre-pandemic world—written in 2017 and released into the world in 2018. In the introduction to the first edition, we said we weren't worried about the book becoming dated and obsolete, and we still aren't. Yes, the tools and technologies we have available to us have changed and improved. Yes, the work of work and the global nature of it has changed. And yes, we lived through a pandemic that altered nearly everyone's conception of what work is and what is possible. The lessons learned from the pandemic supported, more than challenged, our contention that location is less important than the leader's mindset.

But the premise, purpose, and need for this book hasn't changed.

Our premise:

Leading a team at a distance is first and foremost about leadership, and the principles of leadership haven't changed—they are principles. What has changed is that people are working in different places and perhaps at different times. Given this, how we apply the timeless principles of leadership in this new world matters a great deal—for the team members working at a distance, for you as their leader, and for the organization that you all serve.

This book is about both those principles and the nuances that matter so much.

Although we need to adjust to lead in a world with more distance between team members, far more won't change. We plan to show you both the principles and the nuances and help you recognize the difference.

This premise leaves us with a few things to clear up before we begin in earnest.

Our Starting Point

First, we were leading remotely, teaching, coaching, and working with leaders in long-distance working conditions long before a pandemic arrived and forced everyone to figure some of this out.

Since writing the first edition of this book, we have written two other books in the Long-Distance Worklife Series—*The Long-Distance Teammate* (in 2021) and *The Long-Distance Team* (in 2023). Those books may well round out the insights and skills you and your team need to be most successful in the future of work. As a reader of this book, you have access to other tools and downloads—all have been updated and refreshed for the way we work today (and will continue to be if the world changes in other important ways).

What Is Leadership?

More is being written about this topic than ever before, and still we need to set the context, since the words *leadership* and *leading* are both in the title of the book. Here is what we believe:

Leadership is present when people choose to follow someone toward a desired future outcome.

So...

You are only leading if people are following.

There is a lot in those two short statements. Let us unpack it a bit more by sharing some truths and myths about leadership.

Leadership is complex.

In visiting with leaders from NASA (a.k.a. rocket scientists), Kevin asked which was more complex—rocket science or leadership. The response was swift and simple—leadership was the clear and decisive winner. The group explained that in the world of building rockets, they can determine the right answer; they know the equations and formulas. They explained that if they put the right numbers into the right formulas, and at the right time (and check their math), they will get the right answer.

In visiting with leaders from NASA (a.k.a. rocket scientists), Kevin asked which was more complex—rocket science or leadership. The response was swift and simple—leadership was the clear and decisive winner.

But as a leader, you are dealing with *people*—people are inherently more complex. And the issues, while perhaps not as dramatic as sending a rocket into orbit, are even more dynamic and are seldom black and white. Leadership isn't easy or simple. And, like rocket science, to become a skilled leader requires study and practice. When we add the complexity of leading people in different locations, it becomes even more complex.

Leadership is an action.

Leadership is typically considered a role, or a person: that is, "They are the leader." While the dictionary says leadership is a noun, leading, the actions that define leadership, is a verb. Leadership is not really something that we have or possess; it is something that we *do*. When you think about leadership, think about actions and behaviors. The point of this book is to answer the question: What are the actions and behaviors that help us help our teams (specifically remotely) get better results?

And if leadership is an action, that means it *isn't a title or position*. You are a leader when people follow you—if they aren't following, you aren't leading. The actions of others aren't guaranteed by a job title, the color of your desk, or the size of your office. A title that proclaims you a leader doesn't make you a leader any more than calling a lion a zebra creates black stripes.

Think of it this way: chances are you have observed or worked for a person with a leadership position who wasn't really leading; alternatively, you know people who don't have or don't want the leadership position, but people are choosing to follow them anyway. It is action, not titles, that make leaders.

Leadership is a responsibility.

When you were placed in or accepted a formal or informal role of leadership, you received a significant amount of responsibility. This may seem obvious if your title is president, CEO, or business owner, but your responsibility is massive as a first-level leader too. Think about it this way: outside a person's closest family and friends, you, as their boss, are about the most influential person in their life. You have an impact on their pay, their work environment (even if you aren't sitting in the same location), the level of stress they experience, the amount of satisfaction they find in their work, and a hundred other things.

People are looking to you. If you are leading, people are *following* you. You have a responsibility, therefore, for more than yourself and your own results. You must make sure that the direction you are headed in is a useful and valuable one. You can try to ignore this responsibility, but it won't change the significance of the role.

And while it is a responsibility, *it isn't a power grab*. Leaders, through their actions, may have a great deal of influence, and therefore, a certain amount of power. But the behaviors that lead to others granting you "power" don't come from your wanting power. They come from your relentless focus on serving others. If you try to grab power, you aren't leading. When you are leading in the ways we discuss throughout this book, much "power" will likely be granted to you.

Leadership is an opportunity.

Nothing positive happens in the world without leadership. The opportunity to make a difference is huge and exciting. Whether you are thinking about the difference you can make for your team, your customers, your organization at large, the communities where you work and live, or even about changing the world, it all requires leadership.

When you exhibit the behaviors of leadership, you are actively trying to create new results that will make a difference in the world. Few things hold greater opportunity than this. Always remember that you have an opportunity to make a difference. A big reason why we wrote this book is to help you make that difference with a far-flung team.

Leadership isn't a gift from birth.

Leadership skills aren't doled out in the genetics of some while others are left wanting. All of us are given a unique bundle of DNA that can allow us to become highly effective, even remarkable, leaders. Do some people have innate strengths that help them as leaders? Of course, but so do you—even if your strengths are different. None of that matters, though, if we don't use those strengths and improve in areas that are harder for us. Few things are sadder than unfulfilled potential. Leadership success isn't nearly as much about genetics as it is about learning and improvement.

Leadership isn't management.

The skills of management are focused on things: processes, procedures, plans, budgets, and forecasts. The skills of leadership focus on people, vision, influence, direction, and development. Both skill sets are valuable, and it is likely that you need all these skills to be successful in your role. While we are not downplaying the management skills, recognize that you are reading a book titled *The Long-Distance* Leader (not *The Long-Distance* Manager); therefore, our focus is on leadership throughout this book. The differences are clear but not distinct: think of the skill sets as overlapping circles like those in the Venn diagram (Figure 1). We need to exhibit both sets of skills, but great leaders aren't necessarily great managers and vice versa.

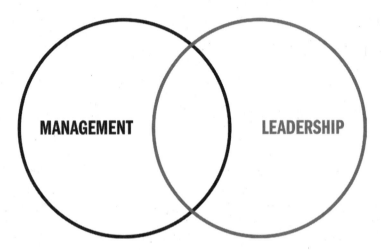

Figure 1: Two Parts of Your Role

To make the point further on the difference between leaders and managers, consider these lists to clarify the differences:

Some Skills of Management	Some Skills of Leadership
■ Coordinating	■ Collaborating
■ Planning	■ Coaching
■ Forecasting	■ Guiding
■ Budgeting	■ Communicating
■ Sourcing	■ Team building
■ Directing	■ Creating change

Some Skills of Management	Some Skills of Leadership
■ Maintaining	■ Providing vision
■ Problem solving	■ Supporting
■ Setting objectives	■ Encouraging
■ Being tactical	■ Setting goals
■ Focusing on the business	■ Being strategic
■ Creating incremental improvement	■ Creating purposeful disruption
■ Doing things right	■ Doing the right things
■ Attending to details	■ Focusing on people
■ Focusing on processes	■ Thinking (and talking about) the big picture

While neither list is comprehensive, notice that all the behaviors in both lists are important; to be at your best, you will be capable of all of them. Hopefully the lists make our point that the skills *are* different yet complementary. To be clear, this book spends far more time on the skills and behaviors on the leadership list.

Remember, this book is about leading at a distance, which means we talk about some critical leadership principles to provide context for what changes when we're leading remotely. This book isn't a complete treatise on leadership, so if you are looking for that, you are reading the wrong book. If you want or need more grounding on leadership principles, we suggest you start with or supplement your reading of this book with some of the books noted in "Recommended Reading" toward the end of this book.

With this solid foundation, we are ready to get started. Let's begin with what we have learned, and are learning, about Long-Distance Leaders.

Pause and Reflect

Ask yourself these questions:

▶ What are my beliefs about leadership?

▶ What is my personal balance of skills and focus between management and leadership?

Part I

Getting Started

Ask yourself if what you are doing today is getting you closer to where you want to be tomorrow.

—Anonymous

Chapter 1

What We Know about Long-Distance Leaders

Rule 1: Think about leadership first, location second.

Leadership is about making others better as a result of your presence and making sure that impact lasts in your absence.

—Sheryl Sandberg, American technology executive, philanthropist, and writer

Eric is a really solid manager, and before the pandemic, he had a traditional team in place. Since then, his team has become hybrid, with people working from home several days a week. On the surface, everything's fine, but as he told us, he spends too much time worrying about what he doesn't know, or what might be happening, rather than on the work itself. He second-guesses himself more than ever and feels less confident in his decisions. As he says, "I think it is going okay, but I'm sure I and the team aren't nearly as effective as we could be."

There are a lot of people like Eric.

If you're reading this, you agree with us that "okay" or "not terrible" isn't nearly good enough. Leadership is aspirational; no one who picks up this book wants to be merely average or normal. You want to be an excellent leader and, if possible, to achieve that with far less stress than you're feeling now.

When we wrote the first edition of the book, we felt we needed to state the case that leading at a distance was different, complex, and important. We talked about our research and experience. Now, millions of leaders and teams have had this experience. We don't need to state research; you have your own experience. Here's what we all know now.

The challenges of leading at a distance are different in nuanced ways from those of leading in physical proximity. All leaders (regardless of working situation) need to coach, give feedback, set clear expectations, communicate, provide direction, and a hundred other things. *What* we do as leaders hasn't changed. *How* we lead must.

Added to that, if your team is in any of the hybrid approaches, your job may be more complex and harder than when everyone was always working remotely. And even if your organization seems to be settling into (or trending back to) mostly onsite work, you will likely always have a hybrid component to your team.

Even on teams that are ostensibly co-located, leaders are experiencing "backdoor" hybrid work—team members are taking advantage of flexibility to work from home or remotely more often than is officially allowed. While this type of work can help maintain morale and team engagement, it does complicate getting the work done.

If you have a single person remote even part of the time, you are leading at a distance. Stated another way: unless you are leading on the front line of a shop floor, a hospital, a hotel, a warehouse, or a restaurant, you are a Long-Distance Leader.

This book is about mindsets and skillsets you need to successfully lead at a distance. Before we get to the details, though, let's discuss some overall things we've learned that provide context for everything that follows.

Let Go and Lean In

Long-Distance Leaders need to let go of some things and lean into some others. Here's what we mean.

We need to let go of these things:

- *Our need for control.* Many of us struggle with this. We feel things are out of control when we can't see our team. If we can't see them, how do we know if they are working?

- *Our focus on activity.* Related to control is the erroneous belief that productivity equals activity. Worrying about the time it takes someone to change out their laundry while they should be at their laptop is folly. The amount of effort people have put into looking like they are working is time far better spent thinking about or doing the required work.

- *Our skepticism.* It is human nature: when we can't see things, we often assume the worst. Those less-than-rosy assumptions about our team members create cynicism and erode trust.

We need to lean into these:

- *Trust.* Much of the ongoing debate about where people should work comes down to trust. Leaders who trust their team members and work to build that trust are far more likely to build effective Long-Distance Teams.

- *Empathy.* If there is one thing the pandemic should have taught us as leaders, it is that we can be empathetic with our teammates. And when we are (pandemic or not), we are far more effective as leaders.

- *Clearer expectations.* When the work expectations are mutually clear between leaders and their teammates, greater success follows. This truth is even more important when people and their leaders are working at a distance. Clarity supports better results, less rework, and higher levels of trust.

- *Intentionality.* Perhaps the biggest change we must make as Long-Distance Leaders is being more intentional about many things. You will see this theme in nearly every chapter of this book.

Model the 3Ps

In our book *The Long-Distance Teammate*, we introduced the 3P Model of Remote-Work Success that outlined three factors that support the success of any person working at a distance (see Figure 2). These three factors apply to leaders as well. In fact, leaders must exhibit them for themselves and support them for others.

Figure 2: The 3P Model

Modelling the 3Ps as a leader looks like this:

- *Understanding productivity.* As we hinted earlier, productivity isn't about activity, it's about accomplishment. Productivity isn't working more hours or writing or answering emails when you could be spending time with your family (or sleeping). Are you getting more of the right things done?

- *Being proactive.* Being proactive means being intentional. Are you proactively doing important but not urgent things like having one-on-ones, reaching out to check in with your team members, being available, and coaching? Or are you just floating through your workdays moving from one meeting and task to the next?

- *Recognizing potential.* When we can't see people, their skills and potential might not be as obvious. Do you see the potential people possess? Are you actively helping people develop and grow? Are you doing this for yourself too?

If you have a single person remote even part of the time, you are leading at a distance.

Apply the 3C Model

In our book *The Long-Distance Team*, we introduced the 3C Model of Team and Culture Design (Figure 3). Too often in hybrid or remote teams the team aspect is ignored, downplayed, or forgotten. Work is still done by groups working together, even if they never see each other. These 3Cs define the current culture of your team and can help you move and advance your culture as well. Although we won't teach this model here (your copy of *The Long-Distance Team* will help with that), the importance of these 3Cs will be seen throughout.

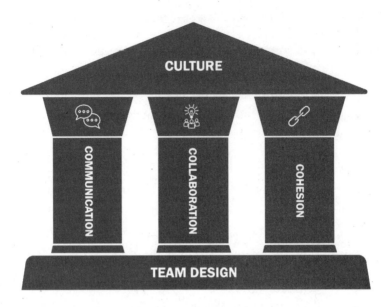

Figure 3: The 3C Model

Applying the 3Cs looks like this:

- *Mastering communication.* Communication was hard before we added distance, technology, and more to the mix. Building communication skills as a leader is critical to your success. We will describe many specific communication skills and habits here.

- *Improving collaboration.* Collaboration is different when people can't gather in person. But it can still be successful. After all, we have written three books (and now a second edition) from different parts of the country. Helping your team understand when and how to collaborate at a distance is critical to team success.

- *Emphasizing cohesion.* Even if people work from home, they crave cohesion, connection, and relationships personally and professionally. As leaders we must support and facilitate this.

Some Important Things to Remember

As you read through the rest of this book, here are some important things to think about:

- While it has become far more common, remote leadership has always existed and will not go away; it can be done well, and you can do it.

- A 2024 Gartner survey revealed that 56 percent of employed adults work from home at least some of the time: 22 percent work fully from home and 34 percent keep a hybrid schedule.[1]

- Leading at a distance is still leading—and while far more has remained the same, you must acknowledge and address the differences between leading at a distance and in person to have the success you want and that your team deserves.

- You can learn, develop, and replicate the skills you need to communicate, influence, build strong working relationships, and engage with people throughout the organization, but only if you understand the dynamics at work and identify the skill gaps in order to mindfully address them.

- It's not just you. The very questions, doubts, and concerns that brought you to this book are simultaneously challenging millions of other smart, talented, dedicated—and exhausted—leaders.

Pause and Reflect

Ask yourself this question:

▶ What are my biggest challenges in leading at a distance?

Online Resource

If you want a clear picture of how you are leading, including the nuances of doing it at a distance, you can learn more about our Leadership 360 Assessment at KevinEikenberry.com/360, or use this QR code.

Chapter 2

The Evolution of Long-Distance Leadership and Hybrid Work

Rule 2: Accept the fact that leading remotely requires you to lead differently and keep learning.

There isn't anything that should ever be considered permanent,
as everything is evolving or changing in some way.

—Steven Redhead, professor and author

Patty has been leading for a long time. She worked with the same team for several years before the pandemic, with everyone in the same location. A big part of everyone's social activity revolved around work. Then the lockdowns happened. Her organization has determined that hybrid work is their future, so people only come to the office the prescribed three days a week—except for the folks who moved and were hired further away—they are nearly fully remote. She had hoped things would have settled down by now, but settled hardly describes how the team feels.

Being a leader has never been simple. The struggle to be effective, to achieve your (and your organization's) goals, and to help the people you lead reach their potential is constant. It's a challenge, and you've accepted, so get on with it.

Not surprisingly, this is a new chapter for the second edition of this book. After all, the first edition was written when people thought of *corona* as a beer or the atmosphere of the sun, not a virus. In 2018, we saw the coming changes as an imminent evolution. The lockdowns of 2020 were cataclysmic. As they relate to work—the when, where, how, and even why have changed forever.

Let's step back, take a breath, and look at the progression of the Long-Distance Worklife.

It might be easy to forget, but people have led at a distance for a very long time, it just hasn't been the norm. During his reign, Genghis Khan ruled half the known world and never held a single Zoom meeting. The sun never set on Queen Victoria's British Empire, yet there's no recorded instance of a single conference call. And they did it without email!

The truth is that while there have been significant changes to the way we lead, the act of leadership itself hasn't really changed all that much.

Now let's fast forward. The first experiments with the shortened work week began in the 1860s, but it wasn't until the Great Depression that the nine-to-five, forty-hour work week at a fixed workplace became the norm. Until recently, workers grew up with this vision of what work looks like.

Nearly eighty years later (in 2018), we wrote the first edition of this book and talked about the growing trend, aided by technology, of people working remotely. It wasn't new, but it wasn't mainstream either. We highlighted some other changes that had facilitated this experimentation, things like:

- *The significant shift to written communication.* Not only did written communication grow, but it was now done by everyone, including leaders, not just by clerks, assistants, or the steno pool.

- *The availability (and widespread use) of email.* Email went from novelty, to useful, to one of the most complained-about parts of work life.

- *Social media's existence and prevalence.* It has changed how people consume content and has shifted the expectations of response times.

- *Web communication platforms.* We began moving from email to other text-based tools, and video conferencing moved from science fiction to our laptops and phones.

Then came the pandemic, and what had been a gradual evolution changed as quickly as you could say "lockdown." Within days we began saying that "the genie is out of the bottle." People who might have been able to work at home on the days they waited for a repairman to show up were now proving they could work from home every day. Because they had to.

Most people say the rate of change today is faster than ever. Wayne wonders, as he surveys all the change since his grandparents were born, if that is technically true; it certainly feels that way. Regardless, things are changing fast. Here is what is undeniably true: what has changed in the workplace since the start of the pandemic feels like it happened at supersonic speed.

Since the start of the pandemic, our view of and what we expect from work have changed, forever. The time we are living in feels confusing, full of compromises, and as Patty says, unsettled. If that is how you feel, it is understandable. This book is meant to help you see things a bit more clearly and navigate to the future more successfully.

What's Next?

Predicting the future isn't easy and we don't know when you will be reading this. While we can't guarantee a perfect picture with all the details of the future of work, we can say some things with great confidence.

- *The future is flexible.* Your children and the society around them won't see work as static nine to five, forty hours a week, onsite. That might still be one reality, but the when as well as the where of work will change.

- *Hybrid is here to stay.* Not for everyone, and not in the same form for every situation. But a world in which a portion of workers regularly work alone sometimes and, at others, in physical proximity to their coworkers will continue to be very common. And while some organizations insist they are an in-office workforce, unplanned and unsanctioned remote work and hybrid arrangements will complicate things.

- *Expectations will change.* Expectations of leaders will continue to evolve and so will those of the team. The most successful leaders and organizations will navigate these changes collaboratively, not by fiat or demand.

- *Technology will continue to evolve.* And not just our web platforms and file-sharing tools; generative AI (and related technologies) will change work in significant ways.

- *The genie isn't going back in the bottle and everyone's not going back to an office or worksite.* While we don't know exactly what the future holds, we know that we will need the skills of leading at a distance and they will be more important than ever.

What Does This Mean for Us?

In a fast-moving world it can be hard to get our bearings. Often, in this sort of uncertainty, we want to toss everything out and start over.

Don't do that.

Before we get caught up in how things are different and how much things have changed, let's take a breath. The truth is that while there have been significant changes to the way we lead, the act of *leadership* itself hasn't really changed all that much.

The changes we are experiencing, as big as they seem, are first-order, not second-order, changes.

What's the difference?

A first-order change means we need *to do the same things but in a different way.* We need to do something faster, smarter, or using different tools, but the task at its root is fundamentally the same. A second-order change implies what we're doing doesn't work at all, and we need to do something *completely different.*

Here's an example. Let's say your salespeople aren't making enough outbound calls. You can buy lists, offer training, change incentives—those are first-order changes.

Or you can outsource outbound calls to a different group, freeing salespeople to handle customers more effectively. That's a second order of change. First order is how it's done, second is what you do.

If you were a leader "in the before times" when everyone was face to face, you may be struggling, even if you have been leading at a distance for some time now. Some of your skills are less valuable now (maybe you were great in face-to-face meetings, for example), and some of the strategies that always worked don't anymore. You might even be tempted to believe that things are returning to "normal," and you can revert to your old habits.

Or maybe you became a leader for the first time during all this cataclysmic change. You had to learn on the fly (like many new leaders do) but alone and without mentors who knew how to navigate these new challenges.

Either way, leadership is leadership. But there are differences, and those matter—a lot. We will dive into these later in this book. But remember, what you're experiencing is a first-order change, not a second. *What* you do may not be a problem, but *how* you do it may well be. In the next part of the book, we'll share a model that helps illustrate that fact.

Pause and Reflect

Ask yourself these questions:

▶ How has work changed for me and my team?

▶ What changes do I see coming now?

▶ Have I noticed any changes in my leadership behavior or approach when I am leading at a distance? If so, what are they?

▶ What is the most stressful part of leading people who work apart from me?

▶ What is working well? And what's not?

Chapter 3

What It Means to Lead at a Distance

Rule 3: Know that working remotely changes the interpersonal dynamics, even if you don't want it to.

Sometimes when I consider what tremendous consequences come from little things . . . I am tempted to think . . . there are no little things.

—Bruce Barton, ad executive and US congressman

Ahmed had been a supervisor for a couple of years before 2020; his team had been right down the hall. Since the pandemic, three of his team members have continued working from home. He knows the world has changed but doesn't really understand what leading a hybrid team will mean for him long term and what he must change as a leader. He's often surprised at how little misunderstandings turn into problems and how people miss messages he thought were perfectly clear.

In this chapter, we are going to talk more about the distance that you (and Ahmed) are experiencing and what it all means. We are going to expand on the last chapter to make sure you know where you are and where you want to go. Most importantly, we want you to remember that if even one team member is away from their teammates most of the time, your hybrid team is actually more remote than co-located.

Remote versus Virtual

Here's some basic terminology that will be important as we continue. First, there are *remote* teams and *virtual* teams. These terms are used interchangeably but aren't necessarily the same.

According to Karen Sobel Lojeski[1] of Stony Brook University (SUNY Stony Brook) and now CEO of Virtual Distance International, here's the distinction:

- *Remote distance* is just what it says. The people you lead are somewhere else, at least part of the time. Perhaps you're a sales manager with direct reports working from the road who are constantly on their laptops and phones. Or you're a project lead with team members scattered from Bangor to Bangalore. Or the company you run has a single location, but you have one person who, because of childcare needs, works from home one day a week. These scenarios have become more common post-Covid as we move to normalize hybrid work.

   The important thing about these teams is that team members may not be in physical proximity to each other. They lack the constant visual and other types of cues that frequent interaction and exposure to each other provide. Communication might be constantly mediated by screens and email. Meanwhile, the reporting structure and the power balance is fairly traditional. Things are different, but to a much lesser degree than it felt like at first.

- *Virtual distance* is more nuanced. You and your team members communicate primarily through technology, and you may be separated by distance, but there are also structural differences to relationships in this type of team. If you lead a project in which your team is made up of people from different departments, for example, you may have all the responsibility of a leader but none of the actual authority. Project teams and ad hoc teams are frequently *virtual*; they have a project manager or leader, but that person may have no direct supervisory power—everyone on the team has a "real boss" they report to. This makes influence, rather than authority, the main way to get things done. The traditional levers of power ("I'm the boss, you have to do what I say") aren't as simple as in the past.

Additionally, virtual distance can be emotional. If you have a coworker who would rather send you an email than talk to you face to face, there is virtual distance, even though the "remote distance" is easily covered. Now imagine they are literally out of sight (they couldn't walk to your office if they wanted to)—how much more difficult would it be?

Types of Teams

We also need to be clear about what we mean when we talk about team dynamics. Whether it's a functional team, a project team, or a volunteer team, your team is one of three types:

- *Co-located teams.* Here everyone's working in the same location most of the time. This is the kind of team most of us, at least those over thirty, grew up on.

- *Completely remote teams.* People work together toward a common goal, but they do most of their work physically separated from each other. Most communication then is not face to face. A classic example is a sales manager with one direct report per region.

- *Hybrid teams.* Some of your people share a workspace; others are elsewhere. This might include full-time remote workers, people in other offices, or even those working on a client site. The most common hybrid team exists when people work from home a couple of days a week—or whenever they feel like it. One of the fastest-changing challenges for hybrid teams is that people are constantly changing where they work—sometimes they're in the office, sometimes they're away—so processes and access to information can change almost daily. Remember, hybrid can be more than a presumed compromise. It can be more than just making the best of an awkward situation; it can be a whole new way of thinking about the when, where, and how work is done.

Each of these types of teams has things in common (they need to get work done, exchange information, and build on each other's work) and unique challenges ("management by walking around" doesn't work if you are in Seattle and part of your team is in Sydney or Singapore). But our focus is on completely remote and hybrid teams throughout this book.

Beyond these distinctions, there are further differences for your remote or hybrid teams based on the context of the work. Consider the following:

- *Sales teams.* If you have a team of salespeople, it is likely that you once were one of those salespeople. Sales teams have been doing the remote thing longer, which can mean they experience less pain working remotely, or as we have often found, it just means they don't know how much better it could be. It might also be true that because of their past "remote" experience, they haven't evolved and improved as much as they could have. Competition between team members is natural and needs to be carefully managed to ensure members stay engaged and connected to the team and the organization.

- *Project or ad hoc teams.* These teams may be shorter lived, with high-stakes results on the line. You might be leading a project team and not have some (or any) of the team members reporting to you. The biggest objection to remote and hybrid work for this kind of team is ensuring collaboration and information sharing.

- *Individual contributor teams.* Sales teams likely fall into this category, but they aren't the only example. When you lead a team of individual contributors, the focus on remote teamwork and collaboration might not be as strong, yet you still must keep team members from becoming too insulated or individually minded. They are still on a team, with team goals and objectives.

- *Global teams.* At some point if people aren't in the building, it doesn't matter how far away they are . . . except when cultural differences and vast differences in time zones make communication and relationship-building more challenging.

What Hasn't Changed

When we were first writing this book, Kevin had this question on his whiteboard for several months: *"How does leadership change, and what shouldn't change?"* In many ways that sums up this part of the book, and it certainly is the focus of this chapter.

First, here's what shouldn't change:

- *The leader's primary focus.* Whether your team members are outside your office door, down the hall, out in the warehouse, or in another time zone or country, leadership is still about human beings. Too often leaders want to move to the details of a situation or context without first remembering that team members have feelings, emotions, needs, and personal objectives that the leaders need to consider. Begin with the idea that everything starts with people, and you will start in the right place. This is even more important when your team is fully remote or hybrid.

- *The fundamentals of human behavior.* Since you are leading people, the more you understand the psychology of people—their wants, needs, desires, fears, and anxieties—the more successful you will be.

Contrary to what you might read in the popular or trendy business press, the fundamentals of human behavior have not changed because people work from a different location, use a certain type of technology, or were born in a certain year. Our view of work was changed by the collective experience of the pandemic, but behavioral fundamentals have not changed. We will point to these fundamentals throughout the book.

- *The principles of leadership.* Along with the fundamentals of human behavior, there are skills and characteristics that influence us to follow some people more than others. These haven't changed as people have migrated from the office to their homes or a client location.

- *The roles of leaders.* Regardless of where the team is located, leaders are asked to coach, influence, and communicate. They are expected to coalesce and collaborate with teams, set goals, and lead change. We talked a bit about this in Chapter 1, but it deserves to be restated here: the basic roles expected of leaders haven't changed as team members have dispersed.

- *The high-level expectations of our output.* Our organizations still want us to hit production targets, finish valuable projects, meet the budget, work safely, and a hundred other things. These high-level work goals don't change when people work in different places.

Although these important things haven't changed, we must recognize and address the differences caused by distance or, like Ahmed, we'll experience frustration and unexpected surprises.

What Has Changed

You're reading this book because something has changed dramatically in the way you work. Odds are, it's one or more of the following.

Geography

We've worked with organizations that talk about leading teams on different floors or in different buildings on the same corporate campuses. There is no doubt that some of the long-distance factors we discuss in this book are valid even over short distances. What is changing is how geographically dispersed we have become. Kevin has, for many years, led a team spread across seventy-five miles, but now that team spans from Richmond, Virginia, to Las Vegas, to Phoenix, to Michigan, to South Carolina, to Indianapolis and beyond. Even that isn't as dispersed as what you may face, with teams spanning the globe from Dallas, Texas, to Dubai; from Dublin to Danforth, Illinois. These geographic changes matter, perhaps in different ways than you might think initially.

Many people moved during Covid and now live further from the office than before. That extra distance can create pressure to move to hybrid work or allow remote work more often.

Now you don't just have distance but time zones, cultural norms and expectations, and generally more complexity to your work as a leader . . . as if it wasn't complicated enough.

You Are Sometimes Out of Sight

This may seem obvious, but when leading at a distance, you aren't seen as often by the people you want to influence.

It is easier to lead by example if people can see you. If you want others to help each other, you need to let them see you are willing to roll up your sleeves. If you are willing to do the dirty work, people will notice. Those physically around can see that your behavior is consistent with your values.

When you share space with people, they can ask questions on the fly or request a meeting at a moment's notice because your door is open, or they know you are around. People not in the office can't have that awareness, so you must have processes to overcome this difference. What does an open-door policy look like if people can't see the door?

Your physical presence conveys the power of your position and your willingness to lead. If people need to schedule time with you, aren't sure if now is a good time to ask a question, or haven't developed a warm personal relationship with you, you have both immediate and long-term problems to overcome.

On hybrid teams, being seen has an unexpected downside. When the team members get unequal access to you and each other, it can lead to problems. The very nature of hybrid teams, with some in the office most or all of the time and others who are there less often, can lead to miscommunication and the challenge of *proximity bias*—unintentionally favoring team members who are physically close and available to you over those who are more distant.

Whether we're talking actual physical presence or virtual presence where you are available and visible to your people, being seen is critical to leadership and suffers in a long-distance relationship.

Technology

Kevin started his company with a fax machine and internet through CompuServe. Besides letting you know that Kevin has been around a while, this fact reminds us of how much technology at work has changed. Recognizing the technology that is available to you and using it appropriately and effectively can be a big lever for your success as a Long-Distance Leader. Keeping up with new tools that make your work and communication more effective is part of your job.

If you are a Long-Distance Leader, you must encourage the use of the right tools at the right times, and you must use them yourself. If you aren't using the available tools, your team won't either. If they don't have a model of success to look toward because you aren't using the technology at hand well or at all, good luck getting them to use those tools.

Working Relationships

Although people aren't working in the same building or corridor, they still work together, and hand off work to each other, and therefore they must communicate successfully.

Relationships don't develop or improve simply because of regular face-to-face interaction. Personal contact helps create/improve working relationships. The need for working relationships (both practically and psychologically) doesn't change when people work remotely from each other, but the opportunities and context for building those relationships changes drastically. Learning how to build and maintain these relationships is always an important part of your work as a leader.

And . . . *virtual communication changes the interpersonal dynamic, even if you don't want it to.* As a Long-Distance Leader, it gets harder to nurture—and perhaps even more important—to *intentionally* nurture relationships with all your team members.

You Get Fewer Communication Cues

When you speak to someone face to face, you get instantaneous feedback. Some of it is purposeful—people ask questions or comment. Much of this is involuntary; the broad smile of acceptance or the furrowing of a brow that tells us we need to adjust our message, repeat it, check for understanding, or get more information before we proceed. We constantly and naturally adjust our messages on the fly based on those real time responses.

As a Long-Distance Leader, it gets harder to nurture—and perhaps even more important—to *intentionally* nurture relationships with all your team members.

When working at a distance, the balance of communication modes changes. Think about how much of your interaction takes place in writing. Email, texts, and online communication are your most frequent methods of passing information back and forth. That often feels impersonal and cold. It's one-way communication and it demands that you hone all your communication skills, not just your verbal ones.

Technology helps, to be sure. When we use voice-only communication like the phone, our tone of voice and words exist without the supporting evidence of smiles, winks, or posture to help support our message. And even when people can see us (if we're using webcams or videoconferencing), video alone can't completely overcome a conscious separation from our audience.

In a world in which those immediate cues are missing, you must ensure your message is easily understood and that you find other ways to receive critical cues. Sure, you sent that email saying you're changing how the process for the Jackson account is going to work. But does that mean people really have the information they need to adjust or know how this will impact them? Are they blithely accepting the news, or are they freaking out and frantically instant messaging each other while you sit back thinking everything's fine?

We have all spent a lifetime learning to communicate in person—and now we're conducting our most important work in ways that are less natural and require even more of our attention.

Information Gets Filtered

The way information is received is often filtered and mediated in unexpected or unintended ways.

As a leader, you don't just send messages; you receive them . . . in mass quantities and multiple forms. When you work in proximity with people, you can pop in for a clarifying chat or watch their body language as they give you bad news and respond accordingly. When you receive information on the phone, often without context or advance notice, it is hard to make sure you're really reading carefully, processing the information clearly, and responding in ways you are proud of.

Your Approach to Leadership May Be Out of Date

For a lot of us, our first leadership experiences occurred when everyone was in the same location. We could walk through the cube farm and see who was (or at least who appeared to be) working and who wasn't. We overheard conversations or saw actions and could respond proactively and immediately.

Like us, you may have had managers or leaders who relied on the old command-and-control method of getting things done ("Because I said so"). Because they were nearby or could pop in at any moment, they watched everything we did and made sure we did it exactly the way they wanted it done. Whether that was good or bad, it was at least *possible*.

But when your team is scattered to the far corners of the continent, it is impossible to know what every person is doing all the time. Even if you want to monitor absolutely everything they do and make sure people aren't slacking off, you can't do it, and it's important to ask why you even want to. Since you can't know exactly what everyone's doing at any given time, you need to find ways to make sure people have the proper guidance for their tasks, are clear on the metrics, and communicate their progress to you in ways that give you what you need to maintain progress—and your sanity. Stated another way, to lead successfully at a distance, you must build greater trust with and between your team members—command and control won't work and will drive you crazy if you try to continue operating that way.

(Some of) People's Needs Change

The basic needs of humans don't change, but the context of working locations may make some needs more important or obvious than they were in the past. If you have team members working mostly from home, they may have interaction needs previously met in the workplace that now are missing. This can also mean that when people are together, there's more socializing than before. As a Long-Distance Leader, you must notice the needs that surface and find ways to help meet them. Why? Because as those needs are met, people are better able to focus on and complete their work successfully.

This isn't only true for the more extroverted on your team who might miss the interaction and flow of life at the office while working remotely. In this digitally connected world, people have become increasingly isolated from each other physically, and the workplace has been, for many, that oasis of connection. Now, as people work from home, we as leaders must be aware of these needs. Cliques aren't just in high school anymore. They may form more often at work as the people who see and interact with each other create tighter bonds than they do with the teammates they see less often. If we help people meet those needs and encourage them to do so, we not only get more productive team members but healthier and less-stressed ones too.

More Individual Work Focus

Often as people work remotely, their work becomes more focused on individual tasks and individual contributions. This shift to an individual focus and away from the team isn't necessarily bad; in some cases, it probably leads to better results. However, it does need to be recognized by the organization, by us as leaders, and perhaps most importantly, by the individuals doing the work. We must help people see beyond their individual tasks and recognize the need for collaboration and other team-focused work.

Working in Isolation

Leading at a distance is a lonely job.

While it's lovely to have uninterrupted time to get your work done, part of the joy of leadership is being with other people. Hearing other opinions, getting timely answers to questions, brainstorming, and building on ideas is an exciting and rewarding part of your role.

But where do you turn when you have a simple question? Do you have access to trusted advisors when you experience doubt? Can you check your assumptions, or do you come up with an idea and fire off orders without running them by someone close by first? Moreover, you don't get to see the acceptance of your ideas or hear good news firsthand . . . never mind being able to celebrate over pizza or a slice of birthday cake in the breakroom.

Our customers confirm that feeling isolated from their teams is a huge concern for leaders and impacts their effectiveness and job satisfaction. But who are you supposed to turn to for information, inspiration, and companionship in an increasingly long-distance workplace?

Now What?

Yes, being a Long-Distance Leader is difficult. It's also not impossible. (Remember, Genghis Khan and Queen Victoria did it . . . so can you.) You have to think about your job in new ways, be aware of the changing dynamics that impact you and your work, and change some behaviors.

In the rest of this book, we'll look at each of the challenges we face as leaders, how leading at a distance affects them, and the new attitudes, points of view, and behaviors we'll have to apply to these changes.

Pause and Reflect

Ask yourself these questions:

▶ What type of team do I have, and how does that inform how I lead?

▶ How has distance changed the way my team works and my effectiveness?

▶ How has working apart from people changed my approach to leadership?

▶ Which of the changes are impacting me the most?

Part II

Models That Matter

The purpose of models is not to fit the data but to sharpen the questions.

—Samuel Karlin, American mathematician

Chapter 4

The Remote Leadership Model

Rule 4: Use technology as a tool, not as a barrier or an excuse.

All the tools, techniques, and technology in the world are nothing without the head, heart, and hands to use them wisely, kindly, and mindfully.

—Rasheed Ogunlaru, speaker and coach

Alan has been leading successfully for a long time. When the company allowed some team members to work from home and then changed the org chart so Alan had some folks in the Mobile plant reporting to him, neither he nor his boss thought much about it. He knew all the players and they knew him; he knew the work, and he knew how to lead. When IT gave him access to some new technology, he thought, "I don't need that, I have all the tools I need; it's working fine."

So, if being a leader in a remote/hybrid environment isn't *really* all that different, why does it feel lonelier, more stressful, and just plain harder?

After a lot of thought and discussion with remote leaders, we came up with a simple model that conveys a big message. Although it was originally created for purely remote teams, it applies in hybrid situations as well. We call it the Remote Leadership Model (Figure 4).

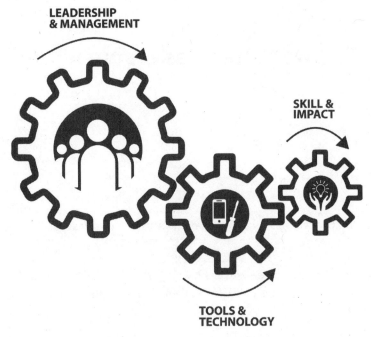

Figure 4: The Remote Leadership Model

The model depicts three interworking gears that function together to propel remote work forward. The largest gear is Leadership and Management, which is the role/work you were hired to do. The second smaller-but-critical gear is made of the Tools and Technology you must use in order to make the work happen at a distance. Finally, the smallest gear is Skill and Impact—the ability to use those tools well. Although it is the smallest gear, you can't ignore it or dismiss its importance.

Let's describe the model in greater detail.

The Leadership and Management Gear

This gear reminds us that our job as leaders—the leadership and management behaviors we are expected to exhibit—is the same as it's ever been. *What* we're supposed to do (the expectations) hasn't changed much since the project manager at the pyramids plied his craft. Regardless of whether our people share a cube farm or are scattered around the globe, these behaviors are the things expected of leaders.

In his book *Remarkable Leadership*, Kevin outlined thirteen competencies that apply to all leaders. To improve in your effectiveness, you must continue to develop in these competency areas:

1. Remarkable leaders learn continually.

2. Remarkable leaders champion change.

3. Remarkable leaders communicate powerfully.

4. Remarkable leaders build relationships.

5. Remarkable leaders develop others.

6. Remarkable leaders focus on customers.

7. Remarkable leaders influence with impact.

8. Remarkable leaders think and act innovatively.

9. Remarkable leaders value collaboration and teamwork.

10. Remarkable leaders solve problems and make decisions.

11. Remarkable leaders take responsibility and are accountable.

12. Remarkable leaders manage projects and processes successfully.

13. Remarkable leaders set goals and support goal achievement.

While you can argue about the specifics on the list, you can't argue that working remotely makes any of these behaviors less important. Furthermore, leading remotely doesn't add much to this rather imposing menu. The responsibilities of leading remain the same whether you're all together or not. The work needs to be done, whether people are outside your office door every day, in the office each Tuesday and Wednesday, or in Guam.

How well you've demonstrated your abilities in these areas is another question for another time, but until the last few years, we've only ever had to really perform our duties in a centuries-old way: together in the same place, and pretty much face to face. This is no longer the case.

The difference lies in the other two gears. Smaller doesn't mean less significant; the old expression "little hinges swing big doors" is as true now as it's ever been.

The Tools and Technology Gear

This intermediary gear is perhaps the most important difference when leading remotely. Leaders are expected to exhibit all the leadership behaviors we've mentioned and do so using tools and technology with which they might not be comfortable. Even if you have been using more tools than ever, this is still a bigger deal than you might think.

If you're an American and have ever driven in England, you've probably risked your life proving this point. At first blush, driving a car is driving a car: four wheels, steering wheel, engine, windshield in the front—it's more than 90 percent the same as driving in your own neighborhood. The only differences are that the steering wheel is on the other side of the car and you drive on the "wrong" side of the road.

These small differences have led to an awful lot of stressful drives and near misses. And it's not just driving. Even walking is impacted by the direction of traffic. The city of London has painted arrows on the streets that basically say, "Hey Stupid Tourist, the bus is coming from the other way—watch where you step." It's a small change that can mean the difference between a carefree vacation and a visit to the emergency room.

How does technology impact your leadership behavior? You likely feel those differences every time you want to ask a complex question but settle for sending an email, or when you know you should have an important coaching session and make do having it on the telephone (where you can't see the happy gleam in the other person's eye or the panicked look on their face). Making a presentation via webinar technology isn't nearly as rewarding as being at the front of an assembled crowd, gaining energy from the audience's laughter and applause.

The job of leading—*what we do*—hasn't changed nearly as much as *how we do it*.

On hybrid teams, there is a complicating factor. Because some people see each other frequently, they often tend to rely on low-tech conversations and ad hoc meetings that unintentionally exclude those who aren't in the office that day. Also, those working outside the mother ship may feel they don't have access to information, answers, and team conversations unless the team leverages technology in new ways. Slack, Microsoft Teams, and more effective and accessible databases are critical if the team is to be a single, cohesive unit.

As we've mentioned, one of the most important changes hybrid work has brought has to do with not just what you do and how, but when you do it. Time zones and flexible schedules mean asynchronous work and tools like Slack and Teams factor into the work more often than ever before.

This gear begs three important questions.

- What tools are available to help get the job done?

- Are you using the right tool for the right job?

- Do you rely too much on the tools you're comfortable with, ignoring a better choice?

As with so much in life, using the wrong tool for the job can be frustrating and diminish your effectiveness. That matters because you have a demanding job as a leader with a lot of things that need to go right. You don't want to be driving on the wrong side of the road, which certainly makes things more complicated, but that's not the only problem.

The Skill and Impact Gear

The third (and smallest) gear is the simplest concept, the easiest one to maintain, yet often the one that can cause the biggest problems. Having a clear idea of what you should do is important, and choosing the appropriate tool for that job is critical. But if you can't use the tool you've chosen effectively, all the hard work and good intentions in the world won't get the job done.

Here are some important statistics:

- Software developers are aware of a rule of thumb that applies to nearly every software tool ever built—80 percent of people use 20 percent of the features.[1] Having a robust tool like Teams doesn't help you overcome the challenges of remote communication if you don't use the features available to you.

- Two MIT Sloan–CapGemini studies show that leaders who use and are comfortable with technology are rated consistently higher in other leadership areas than those who don't. Yet, a huge number—a big majority—don't feel comfortable or confident using the tools themselves.[2]

- In numerous off-the-record, private conversations, both the people who work for well-known software platforms and their resellers have told us the same story. Two-thirds or more of the people who get licenses for collaboration and communication tools never receive any training or coaching, apart from online tutorials, which many people find extremely unsatisfactory. As one reseller put it, "It's like, 'Here's your _____ license. Try not to hurt someone.'" Did you ever get any training for yours?

Not only do we have tools with which we're unfamiliar, we're not using them well. That can undermine our credibility and effectiveness. This is true for anyone trying to communicate today, but for leaders there are additional challenges:

- Leaders are usually more senior in age and/or experience than those they lead, and therefore they might be more resistant to adopting new technology, or at least they are uncomfortable with it at first.

- Even if you want to adopt technology, odds are you are behind the learning curve compared to those you work with/lead.

- There is a paradox at work. If you don't use the tools, you'll look out of touch and incompetent, but if you use the tools poorly, you will still look incompetent and uncomfortable.

The Remote Leadership Model shows that Long-Distance Leadership is more difficult than leading fully in person. You are being asked to do your job in ways you've never done it before, using tools you aren't confident using. The lesson is simple: the job of leading—*what we do*—hasn't changed nearly as much as *how we do it*.

For the rest of the book, we are constantly drawing distinctions between how leading has always been done in the past and how you need to think and act in today's workplace, because that's what's really changed for us all.

Pause and Reflect

Take a moment to look at the Remote Leadership Model and ask yourself these questions:

▶ How comfortable am I with the Leadership and Management gear? On a scale of 1 to 5 (Not Very Effective to Very Effective), what areas from the list of competencies earlier in this chapter do I feel I excel in? What areas require growth?

▶ How comfortable am I with the Tools and Technology gear? On a scale of 1 to 5, what tools are aiding my communication and work (e.g., Skype, Webex, Dropbox)? Which seem to get in the way or do not offer much help?

▶ Has there been a time when I ignored or didn't use a specific technology or tool and now I wish I had? What happened, and what would I do differently next time?

▶ When I lead a hybrid team, how do my available communication tools help the team stay connected no matter where they work? Are there tools or behaviors that are impacting those who work outside the office differently than the team that's in the office every day?

▶ How comfortable am I with the Skill and Impact gear? On a scale of 1 to 5, how confident and competent am I in using communication technology?

▶ Based on these answers, what new skills would I like to develop that will help me become a more effective Long-Distance Leader?

Chapter 5

The 3O Model of Leadership

The greatest leader is not necessarily the one who does the greatest things. He is the one that gets the people to do the greatest things.
—Ronald Reagan, 40th US President

Connie is a new project manager with a team scattered across the Americas. She's a leader who gets the job done but feels the stress of working beyond her comfort zone. Though her project is on time and on budget, she is starting her day earlier to accommodate stakeholders in Asia and scheduling meetings after her children's bedtime. While the team seems to be doing fine, she is tired, cranky, and fears she can't maintain this pace for long. "If this is what leadership is," she asked us, "how long can someone keep it up?"

How would you define or describe leadership?

For many years, Kevin has done an exercise with groups that is both instructive and inspirational. He starts by asking people to individually *define or describe leadership in exactly six words.* Without fail, no matter the location or experience of the groups, two fundamental points come through. The most common understanding is that leadership is about

- *Outcomes* (stated with such words as *goals, mission, vision, objectives,* and *success*)

- *Other people* (stated with such words as *influencing, coaching, communicating,* and *building teams*)

The good news is that people generally agree on what good leadership looks like regardless of where they live and work. Facilitating this exercise over the years has had a profound impact on Kevin and his philosophy about leadership—even though in every case he has been the supposed expert on the topic. It is from his personal experience, as well as from our experiences leading this exercise with people from around the world, that we developed the 3O Model of Leadership (Figure 5).

The good news is that people generally agree on what good leadership looks like regardless of where they live and work.

As you can see from the figure, the 3O Model of Leadership outlines *three* areas of focus all leaders must recognize and use to reach their maximum success.

- *Outcomes*—You lead people with the purpose of reaching a desired outcome.

- *Others*—You lead with and through other people to reach those outcomes.

- *Ourselves*—You can't leave yourself out of this model. While leadership is about outcomes and other people, none of that happens without you, whether you like it or not.

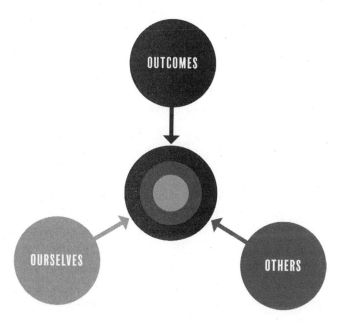

Figure 5: The 3O Model of Leadership

In the story at the beginning of this chapter, Connie was very sensitive to the first two Os. While Outcomes and Others must come first, leaders must also pay attention to the Ourselves component to successfully lead others to the desired outcomes. With good intentions, Connie wasn't supporting herself, and that's where the cracks began to appear in both her confidence and competence.

This model is a more complete picture of the biggest gear in the Remote Leadership Model we shared with you in the last chapter.

Like all models, our 3O Model provides a way for us to clarify and compartmentalize a far more complex world and prioritize our thoughts and actions. We believe this is not just a behavioral model but a mindset.

To lead at your best, you must think of the Outcomes and Others components first. Although the Ourselves component sits in the center of our model, this doesn't imply that you are the most important part of leadership, nor the purpose for it. You are at the core, not the center. Leadership doesn't revolve around you; rather, you bring who you are and how you lead to bear on creating better outcomes for others. This model is meant to show you that while none of this is *about* you, you can't be taken out of the equation either. (Many would call this "servant leadership,"[1] and whether you use that language or not, our belief is that none of us can lead in a sustainably successful way without serving Others and Outcomes.) And while leadership isn't about you, who you are, what you believe, and how you behave are critical to your success.

Now that we have described the model at a high level and put it in proper perspective, let's dive into each of the Os.

Focus on Outcomes

At the highest level, organizations exist to reach outcomes of one sort or another. While it is in vogue for many of these "mission statements" to be a bit esoteric and written in corporate-ese, some of our favorites are more straightforward and make the point here much better:

McDonald's:

> McDonald's brand mission is to be our customers' favorite place and way to eat and drink.[2]

Google:

> Google's mission is to organize the world's information and make it universally accessible and useful.[3]

Of course, we have more than high-level goals. There are all types of goals, objectives, and targets. Sales teams have a quota and product mix that is clearly defined; projects have well-defined metrics for success, including time, budget, and standards.

While some might consider this a management conversation, we disagree. Reaching outcomes is clearly in the overlap between the management and leadership roles. Yes, you must manage the details of the metrics, but you must also attend to the underlying behaviors involved in reaching them.

If we don't focus on outcomes as leaders, we aren't doing what we were hired to do.

The Long-Distance Difference in Outcomes

As a Long-Distance Leader, this focus on outcomes is, if possible, even more important and can be harder. We say that for several reasons:

- *Isolation.* When people work remotely, they are likely alone more of the time than those in the office. (Even if they are on a small team together but remote from you, what follows is still true.) Where we work forms a bubble around our habits, our thoughts, and the things we focus on. This isolation often leads to silos of the smallest nature— people acting as if they are a team of one, a Lone Ranger solving problems and making things happen from their home office desk. Over time, without guidance, they become focused on individual goals and key performance indicators (KPIs) rather than team goals. Leaders want a proactive, driven person working for them (wherever their desk is) but need to help the remote worker see how their outcomes are a part of the larger whole. Our jobs in communicating and clarifying goals can be harder at a distance. In hybrid work situations, those who work remotely might have a perception of favoritism or inequity. "The people in the office get the manager's attention and all the cool assignments." Although this may not be true, it's what it may look like for someone working alone at home.

- *Lack of environmental cues.* When you visit many organizational facilities, you will get a variety of messages about goals and priorities. Whether they're using a slogan like "Quality Comes First," a readerboard with the latest safety statistics, or a list of the corporate goals in every conference room, a common work location provides very clear clues and cues that reinforce important messages that are missing when you work from a home office.

■ *(Potentially) less repetition of messages.* Unless leaders are consistently, and in a variety of ways, communicating and reiterating the goals and outcomes for the team and organization, people may get lost in their own bubble. This is particularly true if you have a matrixed team, where you are the nominal official leader, yet the individuals report to others. Part of your role as a Long-Distance Leader is to find as many ways to keep people focused on the outcomes as possible. We can and should use online portals and other fancy tech tools to do this, but we need to do whatever it takes—personal notes, a whisper in the ear, or carrier pigeons even. You must communicate as often and as creatively as possible to keep all team members on board, in sync, and focused on the goals and objectives of team and organization.

Focus on Others

As a leader, you have a myriad of things that vie for your attention:

■ Budgets

■ Projects

■ Process improvements

■ New product/service development

■ Sales

■ Customer service

■ Margins

We bet at least part of this list resonates with you and that you could add a bunch more to it. You're thinking about all these things, and yet you aren't the one doing most of them.

So how do you overcome the conundrum of lots of important things and not knowing what to focus on?

You focus on something different than anything in the preceding list: *you put your focus on others.*

For example, you focus on the important things we purposely omitted from the earlier list:

- Coaching your team

- Communicating about priorities and projects

- Hiring the right people for your environment, culture, and situation

- Onboarding new team members

- Providing support and guidance

Long-Distance Leaders focus on others. Here are seven reasons why:

1. *You can't do it alone.* Let's start with the most obvious of all—even if you tried, you couldn't do everything that needs doing all by yourself. And if you could, you wouldn't need a team, so you'd have no need for a leader. Leadership is about the outcomes, but those must be reached through others.

2. *You win when they win.* If you're going to focus on others, this has to be the case. You must believe that when you serve others, your needs will be met, your goals will be reached, and you will be recognized appropriately. True and lasting victory comes from helping others win too.

3. *You build trust when you focus on others.* Trust is a powerful lever for team and organization success. When trust is high, job satisfaction,

productivity, and much more is improved. If you want to build trust with others, focus on them and show you trust them first.

4. *You build relationships when you focus on others.* There is a direct correlation between the strength of a relationship and the amount of trust that exists in that relationship. As trust increases, so does the strength of the relationship. Solid working relationships create better results. How do you build a relationship? You express interest in, listen to, and care about others.

5. *You are more influential when you focus on others.* As leaders, we can't force or compel people to take any action, or if we can, it is for a limited time and there will likely be other unforeseen consequences. We can't control people; we can only influence them. Think about it: Who is most successful in influencing you? Someone who you know understands your needs and situation. Someone who wants the best for you. Someone who is on your side of the table. So how can *you* accomplish similar aims unless you are focused on others? Remember, influence is about helping others choose—you want more than mere compliance, don't you?

6. *Team members are more engaged when you focus on them.* This is profoundly true. People want to work with and for people who they know believe and care about them and have their best interests at heart.

7. *You succeed at everything on the list when you focus on others.* Look back at the list of things you need to focus on that we mentioned earlier. If you intentionally and purposefully focus on those around you, will those things all go better? While we're not saying you should ignore or completely delegate those pesky tasks, we are saying that if you focus on others first, the rest will be more successful more of the time.

We could make a longer list of reasons why placing your focus on others is the right choice, but any one on this list is reason enough. Your role as a leader is to aid, support, guide, and help others reach valuable goals and outcomes. When you remember that and focus on them and their needs, you get better results for the organization, the team, and yes, yourself.

The Long-Distance Difference for Others

For reasons discussed throughout this book, maintaining this focus is harder at a distance. Here are some of the reasons why:

Out of sight can be out of mind. Kevin has a tangible example here. Several years ago, Marisa joined our team and worked in an office down the hall from Kevin. This was the context of the working relationship between them, until she got married (to Kevin's son, but we digress) and moved to South Bend, Indiana—about two and half hours away. She worked remotely nearly every day (she came to the Remarkable House—our office in Indianapolis—about once a month to do certain parts of her job). We held everything else static except her work location. For Kevin to be equally as effective at helping Marisa succeed, giving her the resources, time, and encouragement she needed while she was working remotely, he had to be far more diligent, creative, and disciplined. The job got done; it just took more effort and intention.

Happily, about eight months later, her husband (Kevin's son, stay with us) got a new job in Indianapolis, and she was back in the office again. (Now she is one of two hybrid team members, as she comes in one or two times a week if Kevin isn't traveling). Marisa was doing a great job, regardless of her location. Kevin helped her achieve her goals by clearly defining what had to be done, by checking in regularly, and by leveraging webcams and other tools, and Marisa stepped up and became much more independent and self-reliant. That said, is it easier for Kevin to be focused on Marisa's needs and be able to support and coach her from down the hall? Absolutely!

Remember, too, that when some people are in sight (but others aren't)—it's common for leaders to default to the people they see more often.

Your assumptions win the battle.   As a leader, you make assumptions about your people, consciously or not. If you assume they are doing well, you will worry less about them. While this is true regardless of where people work, when you assume all is well and you don't see them, you don't communicate with them (as often). You may assume they'll let you know when they need help or support. You think that no news is good news. Or you worry they will think you are checking up on them if you just want to check in. If you hesitate for any of those reasons, they may (and likely will) take your lack of communication/attention as a lack of focus on them—regardless of your intention. As Long-Distance Leaders, we must understand that when and how we communicate is a scheduling issue and we must make an intentional and conscious decision to do so.

Even if you focus on them, do they know?   The battle between perception and reality will always be won by perception. If your team members don't see the actions that show that you are thinking about them, that you want them to succeed, that you trust them, and more, it really doesn't matter what you are thinking or what your intention is. Kevin has long said, "people watch our feet more than our lips," but when they are remote, they can't watch our feet in a literal sense. If you are to be truly Other focused, you must diligently show it through your actions.

Focus on Ourselves

The great paradox of leadership is that it isn't about us at all—as we have just said, fundamentally leadership is about outcomes and other people.

And yet, who you are, what you believe, and how you behave plays a huge role in how effectively you will do the other things. This is where Connie, most of the leaders we work with, and likely you are encountering the most difficulty.

While this is arguably the smallest of the 3Os, it also in some ways must come first, even though, as the model shows us, we must be last. Or, as we stated before, you are at the core of leadership but are certainly not at the center of your leadership universe.

You might know NFL star Gale Sayers's autobiography *I Am Third*. (If you ever saw the inspirational movie *Brian's Song*, this book was the impetus for that movie. If you haven't seen it, we strongly recommend it. Bring plenty of tissues.) The title came from a line from his friend Brian Piccolo: "God is first, my family is second, and I am third." While our context here is different, the point is similar. While *who* you are and how you lead (Ourselves) can't be denied or ignored, if you think about Ourselves as third, you will serve both Others and Outcomes best.

While you may intellectually agree with what you just read, we need to say a bit more. Some would say it is about how we show up in the world and that since leaders can be successful in different ways, you should lead as who you are. This is true, but only to a point.

You can all bring who you are to your leadership, and many styles can be successful in leading. And we do believe you need to be authentic you, but that isn't an excuse to stay where you are without choosing to change some of your behavior, assess your priorities, build your skills, and get better!

The great paradox of leadership is that it isn't about us at all—fundamentally, leadership is about outcomes and other people.

How you lead starts with what you believe in and think about. Those beliefs and thoughts drive your actions, how you engage with your team, how well you influence them, and ultimately, how they will respond to and perform with you as their leader.

This book talks a lot about what you can do, and perhaps that is why you bought a copy. Ultimately what you want matters, and it's important only in the context of the other two Os—Outcomes and Others.

The Long-Distance Difference for Ourselves

Who you are and how you lead is important wherever your people work, but when you are leading at a distance, some of this is less transparent, and your beliefs and assumptions are even more crucial. Here are three reasons why:

Assumptions (again).   You have assumptions about what it means to work remotely. As organizations struggle to find the right balance of where people should work, they must be aware of their assumptions. For example, if you believe people are less productive at home, do you have data to prove that? If you feel collaboration can only happen around a whiteboard, does your experience really support that? Your assumptions about your team members always impact how you lead. When your folks are working at a distance, there is a very remote chance (pardon the pun) that your assumptions will be challenged simply because you don't see enough evidence to change your mind. You also make assumptions about how much to ask of your people, and how much you're willing to adjust for things like time zones and meeting times. That's where Connie got in trouble—she assumed she solved the problem by working more and taking one for the team. You must identify your assumptions about both yourself and those you lead, challenge them, and revise them when facts dictate.

Intention is important, but not enough.   Throughout this book we talk about being intentional with nearly everything. Here, though, the challenge lies in the gap between what you want and mean to do and what you actually do. Research shows that as humans, we aren't very good at self-assessment, in part because of this gap—we grade ourselves on what we are capable of or mean to do, while others view us based on our actions.[4] As you lead a team remotely, with less-frequent interaction, and when much of that interaction is less rich and robust, it is much more likely that your team members won't see your intention, or will assume the worst, when you aren't quite meeting their needs. They don't know how swamped you are, or that you are stuck in the Des Moines airport; they just know you blew off their one-on-one.

In hybrid teams, we should reexamine how we maximize our time. If your team is expected to be in the office three days a week, perhaps coaching conversations and those one-on-ones are best done when you and your people are in the office already. This might mean rethinking how you schedule these events, but the results will be worth it.

Making a decision. This book will give you lots of ideas to apply—many of them could make a big difference in your ability to lead successfully. None of them will work until you decide to act. As a Long-Distance Leader, you must decide to do the unnatural things, you must focus (even) more on your team members, and you must be diligent in supporting them and their needs, but you can't do those things until you decide that you are going to.

Connecting This to Other Models

We will be the first to admit that there are lots of models of leadership—in fact, elsewhere in this book we referenced Kevin's thirteen competencies of Remarkable Leadership—and all the best models provide a viewpoint into what it means to lead and how to do it well. Humbly, we submit that this 3O Model can sit on top of any of them (or on top of your organization's competency model) to provide an important perspective on them.

Regardless of the skills or competencies, the best leaders will be effectively managing their focus and activity among their 3Os, which are the things that everything about leadership rests on. This overview sets the table for the rest of this book. There is an entire part for each of these Os that will dive deeper and give you specific and concrete ways you can more effectively lead at a distance through the lens of each.

Pause and Reflect

Ask yourself these questions:

- ▶ What do I feel are the most important outcomes expected of me as a leader?
- ▶ How has working remotely impacted those outcomes for me and my people?
- ▶ If my team works in a hybrid way, how am I and how is my team impacted?
- ▶ What do I feel are the most important ways to focus on others in my organization?
- ▶ How has working remotely impacted that focus?
- ▶ How do I see myself in my role as a leader?
- ▶ How has leading at a distance impacted my beliefs and behaviors?

Part III

Achieving Outcomes at a Distance

Successfully working from home is a skill, just like programming, designing, or writing.

—Alex Turnbull, entrepreneur

Part III Introduction

Never mistake activity for achievement.

—John Wooden, Hall of Fame basketball coach

Raul is a new supervisor on a team of software engineers. He works from home and has since before the pandemic, as has most of his team. His manager, though, is back in the office again and continues to worry that team members might not work as hard as they can—or might even be ghost working. His manager constantly asks, "How do you know what they're working on?" or "Are you absolutely positive we'll meet those deadlines?" While Raul trusts his people, he struggles to assure his boss that real work is getting done, even when he can't peer over the cubicle and watch it.

As a leader, you're in the business of reaching desirable outcomes. Helping a team reach such outcomes at a distance is a bit different, so let's start there.

Here are some of the common questions we continue to hear from those leading at a distance:

- What are they doing?

- Are they accomplishing the right stuff (or anything at all)?

- How distracted are they?

- Are they working too much?

Let's come off the ledge, take a deep breath, and look at each of these questions.

What Are They Doing?

While you can't see the people working remotely, do you really know what the people working down the hall are doing either? Are you looking over their shoulders all day? (If you are, perhaps you should start rereading this book from the beginning.) The specific answer here is hard to provide without knowing your industry and the work your folks do, but really, how is it any different whether your people are in the next office or in the next state? Kevin was talking about this question with a client who agreed with him. She mentioned that she used to know someone who came to the office every day and basically spent the day clipping coupons. They looked busy; but clearly, they weren't getting any (work) outcomes! And they were in the office. We can't blame that behavior on being remote.

Are They Accomplishing the Right Stuff (Or Anything at All)?

You should have answers to this as a part of the work process and your role as leader and manager. And this should have nothing to do with where they are working. If you are thinking about this one, you are really thinking about the next question . . .

How Distracted Are They?

The fact is, they are likely less distracted than you or their down-the-hall team members. Before the pandemic, the research agreed that people who work away from the office actually get more done on a task-by-task basis. Some of that is for good reasons (lack of interruptions) and some for not-so-good reasons (they work more cumulative hours). Although working from home is different now (there are more meetings, more use of instant messaging platforms, etc.), no definitive agreement in the research proves people are more distracted (and less productive) at home than in the office.

Even if you don't agree, let's just think about your personal experience. How many distractions and interruptions do you have during a workday in the office? And how many of them are caused by other people in that workplace with you? The distractions and productivity busters that are non-people-related are likely the same for you and your remote folks, but they likely have far fewer people interruptions than you do. Even if one person on your team has trouble working remotely, that does not mean everyone working remotely has the same problem. This is an opportunity for you to coach this teammate, not throw the baby out with the bathwater.

Are They Working Too Much?

This might not be the question you are asking, but you should. When people work remotely (especially from home), boundaries are harder to set. With our phones and devices always within reach, it is easy to check email in the evening (e.g., *Josiah in Jordan could use this, I'll just respond now*), or first thing in the morning—you get the idea. In fact, it's frequently a bit of a vicious cycle: *Mary wants to look like she's working, so she answers email as soon as she gets up in the morning and does it again after the kids are in bed.* No wonder she's getting more done—she's putting in more hours. Is that what you really want?

During the pandemic we routinely asked people how they were using the time they used to spend commuting. While answers like time with family, personal development, and sleep were on the list, the most prevalent answer by far was "working." Emails got answered before they were out of bed and answered long after the kids went to bed. It didn't (necessarily) mean they were getting more done, but they were working more hours.

Understanding whether people really are working harder or longer, or just time-shifting some activities, is important, especially if you have a hybrid team with some in the office and some working from home. Perception can be a significant problem: if Gina, who works in the office, sees George sending emails at all hours, she may decide she needs to stay later or take her laptop home. Conversely, if George is working from home at 8 p.m., but the people in the office stop answering emails at 5 p.m., he might wonder why they are all slackers.

We'll talk more about managing ourselves in Part V, but make sure you are setting reasonable expectations and boundaries for the team around expected response times, working hours, and working on the weekend.

The Real Issues

If these questions (or ones like them) bother you, there are likely three reasons:

- *You are focused on activity, not accomplishment.* Think about this question: Which is more important, how long or hard people work or that the work is done correctly and completed on time? After all, it's the results (outcomes) we want. The previous questions focus on what or how people are doing work, not on if they are getting quality work done. This may be a big focus change for you; even if you agree intellectually, you might have trouble with this in practice. Kevin, while teaching and believing strongly in staying focused on results, has fallen victim to this thinking often. While he has rarely set standard working hours for team members, he's a morning person. It sometimes bothers him when someone comes to work (or logs in) later than he would. Then he remembers this important distinction and recognizes that the quality of the work is the right measure of success. Since it doesn't matter if that copy gets written at 9 a.m. or 6 p.m. as long as it's done by Friday's meeting, why does he concern himself with it? Getting clear about this is important: your job is to support people in getting the right work done in a quality way in the pre-scribed timelines. So why should it matter if they are doing their laundry during the workday, as long as the work is getting done well and the rest of the team doesn't suffer as a result?

- *You think you would be distracted so you are projecting that on others.* You may be someone who struggles in the quiet environment of work-ing from home or who needs the structure of getting in the car and going to the office. If so, that is fine (and yes, routines can be built to overcome some of those challenges if need be), but that doesn't mean everyone struggles just because you do, or you did once.

- *You fundamentally believe that when the cat's away, the mice will play.* If you believe that people only work effectively when supervised, you are going to be hampered in leading any team, regardless of where, when, and how they work. Do you think that just because you aren't there, they are goofing off? Remember: if they are getting the work done, what are you really worrying about?

Oh, and here is one more really important reason:

- *You have a perceived need for greater control.* Underlying at least some of the preceding issues is this fundamental point: if you are worried about your ability to lead remote team members to successful out-comes, you might have control issues. If people have been well trained, have the tools and resources they need, and have your sup-port, they will be successful. If you struggle with control and tend to micromanage, you will be more challenged with leading remotely (and if you get that feedback consistently, you *are* micromanaging even if you don't think you are).

If you were nodding your head at any of these items, we have some sugges-tions for you.

How to Improve

Just because your team acts a certain way, doesn't mean it can't be improved. Work with your team to get the outcomes you all desire.

Build processes together.   Job aids, procedures, checklists, and proven templates to help people do the work are key to achieving good performance. They're critical in a remote environment, where people can't easily watch and learn from their peers. When people have input into what these processes are, they are more likely to be engaged, successful, and committed to the outcome. For a good leader, these processes may provide clues to people's progress and status; in other words, they may be a predictive measure of progress and accomplishment.

Create mutually clear expectations.   It is important to define and agree on the expectations of the work and the results—and how you'll measure success. When people realize their peers are committed to responding before the end of the day, they're less likely to be sitting around fuming when they don't get an immediate response. Also, when people are part of creating the ground rules and expectations, they take responsibility for abiding by them and being better teammates. This is especially important for project teams, where people depend on input from each other on a regular basis. But even on sales teams, where it often feels like every person for themselves, shared outcomes help keep everyone connected and reduce the perception of favoritism.

Change your belief.   Listen to the research, pay more attention, and you will likely change your perspective on the productivity of people who are working at a distance. They will likely be very productive, especially if you have taken our advice.

Reduce your need for control.   We know that may be easier to say than do, but we encourage you to think about what you can influence rather than what you can control. Make sure people have the skills and training they need, provide them with feedback and encouragement, give them resources and tools to be successful, and then *let them do their jobs*. And beyond those actions, repeat after us: let it go.

Chapter 6

Types of Outcomes

Rule 6: Leading successfully requires achieving goals of many types.

People with goals succeed because they know where they are going.

—Farl Nightingale, speaker and author

Angela leads a team of customer service reps, most of whom work from home. Each of those people has individual goals, including the number of calls they take a day, how many calls they personally resolve, and how many they need to escalate to a manager. The reps are also encouraged to share experiences and best practices and let each other know where to find the information they need in a hurry. Sharing and brainstorming happen more among the people in the office than those who are completely remote. Angela has noticed that while individual metrics are being met, few people use the shared file sites or answer each other's questions. So, while some of the goals are clearly met, overall team communication isn't what it should be. When everyone worked in the call center, she didn't have this problem, and she's not sure what to do about it now.

It is one thing to say (or write) "leadership is about outcomes"; but it isn't specific enough to be helpful. After all, in an organization we are trying to reach lots of different outcomes. As Long-Distance Leaders, we need to be aware of, think about, and help our teams reach all of them.

Don't just nod in agreement with the following descriptions; read them like a checklist. Ask yourself how much you focus in each area, and how often your conversations with your team members touch on each of these types of outcomes.

Organizational Outcomes

There are reasons your organization exists; and if you, your team, and the organization collectively aren't performing well enough, you might not get such a good outcome! Depending on the size of your organization, as a leader, you might be involved in setting these organizational targets, or you might only be responsible for understanding these targets and helping your team reach them.

For example, if you work in a smaller organization, you might be in the meeting where the organizational goals for the year are set. If so, your level of understanding (and hopefully commitment) to those goals should be strong. If you are a middle manager in a Fortune 500 company, you likely weren't at the retreat where these goals were set, but your need to understand and communicate them successfully is no less important.

Regardless of how the targets are set and who sets them, as a leader you must make sure your understanding of them is crystal clear so you can help your team members (individually and collectively) achieve them. The bigger your organization is, the more levels might exist (e.g., division, business unit) between you and the full organizational targets. It's your responsibility to understand, communicate, and align the work of your team with these targets, however many levels of them there might be. Consider these questions:

- How clear are these targets?

- How often do you think about them?

- How often does your team discuss or review these targets to track progress?

Team Outcomes

There are larger organizational targets, some of which paint the big picture, but they might seem a bit esoteric to your team. Team outcomes are the specific targets your team is responsible for achieving. While your role in creating organizational targets will vary with the size of your organization and your culture, at the team level this responsibility rests squarely on you. We've worked with leaders in nearly every type of organization, and far too often team targets are weak. We find the reasons include these:

- *They are assumed.* "Everybody knows what our goals are."

- *They are too vague.* "Get the product out the door," isn't really a goal.

- *They are under-reviewed.* "We talked about those last December at the annual meeting."

When your team is in the same location, you catch side conversations, hear parking-lot banter, and have many ways to reinforce and clarify the goals. When you have team members working on their own, these clarifications don't happen easily. You may find discrepancies in understanding and engagement between people who are mostly remote and those who are in the office more often. People must know how what they do fits into the work and success of the team. Ask yourself these questions:

- How clear are our team targets?

- Do all my team members know these targets?

- Are there signs my team members might be confused about these goals?

- How often am I reviewing progress?

Personal/Individual Outcomes

People need to know what outcomes they're responsible for, what targets they are shooting for, and what qualifies as success. Even when people are integral parts of a team effort, they need individual targets to shoot for. Think about this from a sports perspective. The team has an organizational outcome in mind (winning a championship), team results (wins and losses), and perhaps results for a portion of the team (offense, defense, or some subset of the larger team). And yet even with all those outcomes, individual players need targets as well (personal objectives measured by individual performance or statistics). In addition to the short-term targets, they must be thinking beyond their role to their overall career development. As leaders we have a role to play there too.

Leaders must be concerned with both team and individual results. Too often individual goals become the sole focus for the remote team member. Collaboration is harder when you're working remotely; it simply doesn't happen as easily or organically. Leaders need to be aware of this and help facilitate this communication.

Setting clear, mutually understood expectations with team members is one of the most important things you can do as a leader.

Remember that working remotely can be like living alone on an island. Without solid, clear targets, individuals can drift, losing sight of both the big picture and their individual role. That's why tools like Slack/Teams, chat groups, and online project management tools are so important—they provide visibility even when people are miles apart, and they provide consistent information no matter where people work on a given day.

One more thing here too: team members who are "on their island" may be less aware of the individual contributions, roles, and goals of their teammates. When people don't have any clue about the work of others, they are less likely to understand the questions they get from them. It's easy to assume they aren't busy, or that their work isn't important, and much more. This lack of awareness and understanding can cause team rifts, poor communication, frustration, and conflict. As leaders, it is our responsibility to ensure people hear about the good work of their peers and get a chance to build trust in each other. It doesn't matter if you are busy, or if it is hard to do, this is one of the remote leadership challenges you must accept.

As a Long-Distance Leader, make sure that your remote team members have context for the roles and targets of all their teammates. You also need to decide how often you'll check in with each team member on these metrics. This will help you keep your remote team members from feeling either abandoned or micromanaged.

But Wait, There's More

We've just described the core list of the outcomes that a leader in any type of organization must be aware of; we've talked about the results that need to be achieved. But there is a more granular and more operational type of outcome we haven't even mentioned yet.

When you think about outcomes, you likely think about results, and you would probably call what we have just described as *goals*. Goals are important and we are going to talk about how to set them with a remote or hybrid team in upcoming chapters. But these goals are only one type of outcome we need to discuss. On a daily working basis, *expectations* may be more important than goals.

Expectations aren't just about the "big G" goals, or the "what needs to happen." They are about how the work gets done; the rules for working together, the way you'll support and help each other, what tools you'll use, and what good communication looks like.

Clear, mutually understood and agreed-to expectations are the necessary foundation for successful performance—and a more successful (calmer and less-stressed) you. In other words, when people understand clear expectations, they are more likely to succeed. Furthermore, the chances that the outcomes are achieved increases.

When Kevin starts workshops, he usually does an exercise to get people to clarify their goals and expectations for the learning experience. It involves writing down and sharing those ideas with others. In the debrief that follows, the group identifies some important points about expectations that directly apply to our work:

- *Expectations provide clarity.* They become clearer when they're written down. Are the expectations you have of your team members written down, or assumed?

- *Expectations provide focus and set priorities.* They help people be clear on what is most important among the list items. Do you have folks who have mismatch expectations to yours on the most important or relevant parts of the work?

- *Expectations provide context.* Sharing the expectations verbally helps everyone understand, both their own expectations and those of the others in their group. This helps eliminate silos within the team. Have you talked with your people about their expectations?

- *Expectations must be mutually and explicitly agreed to.* Unless you have explicit agreement, people are left to make their own assumptions, and the less frequently they interact, the more likely you'll have a disparity in expectations. Remember that simply sending an email without discussion doesn't guarantee true clarity or agreement.

How can your team members meet your expectations if they don't know what they are?

Before you think everyone on your team has to know your expectations of them, let us ask you another question.

As you read this, are you thinking about a member of your team who you really want to "fix"? Have you been reading in part to see how you can lead that one person more effectively?

If so ask yourself this question:

Do they know what you expect of them?

Because, just like Kevin's workshop situation, if they don't know what you expect, how can they possibly deliver?

Setting clear, mutually understood expectations with team members is one of the most important things you can do as a leader. In doing so, you are performing the simplest thing you can to improve the chances they will achieve the desired outcomes of their roles. The importance of doing this for the success and confidence of team members and for your own sanity can hardly be overstated.

If only part of your team is remote, setting clear goals may be even more important (if that is possible). With some team members in close contact with each other daily, and others out on their own with less interaction, you may get conflicting priorities or misunderstandings. Leaders must help guide and set expectations. In our experience, many leaders aren't doing this very well with their team members down the hall either. If you invest the time in your team to help goals become clear to them, regardless of work location, you are giving them a much clearer picture of the outcomes that will make them successful.

Pause and Reflect

Ask yourself these questions:

- ▶ Are my organizational outcomes clear?
- ▶ Are my team outcomes clear?
- ▶ Are the individual outcomes with each team member clear?
- ▶ Are expectations within my team clear?
- ▶ If my team is hybrid or blended, have I discussed specific challenges like access to information, collaboration, and asynchronous work?
- ▶ If not, when will I start?

Online Resources

To assess how clear and aligned your team is on goals, register at LongDistance Worklife.com/Resources and request the Team Goal Clarity Tool.

To build more effective remote work routines when people don't go to an office, register at LongDistanceWorklife.com/Resources and request the Building Remote Work Routines Checklist. Or use this QR code to register for either tool.

Chapter 7

Setting (and Achieving) Goals at a Distance

Rule 7: Focus on achieving goals, not just setting them.

Setting a goal is not the main thing. It is deciding how you will go about achieving it and staying with that plan.

—Tom Landry, Hall of Fame football coach

Frank has been a sales manager for eight years. He had a hybrid team since before it was cool—he had reps in the field, and others working from the office who sometimes were out with customers. Now his people are working from home more and coming into the office less frequently. His top performers are still making quota, and many are nailing their goals, but he's noticing that newer hires struggle. He's spending more time with them, but they aren't getting the benefit of the war stories and the advice of the seasoned reps that used to happen naturally when people worked together. While the team's total number still looks good, he's spending way more

time managing individual salespeople and not enough working on strategic plan-
ning. He's spending more time on goals he used to be able to set and forget.

In our opinion, there is a major gap in the literature around goal setting. Pick up any book about the subject (you know, the one gathering dust on your shelf), and you will find it does a fine job of outlining a very specific process for setting goals. This usually isn't the problem. The problem is that most of these books don't focus on how to achieve the goals you painstakingly set.

The problem organizations face mirrors our problem with all the goal books: the focus is all on *setting* the goals, when it should be on achieving them.

This plays out in organizations and on teams everywhere. The organization has a deadline for when annual goals will be set. Work and focus is placed on this goal-setting process, with meetings slipped into time blocks where the "real" work is normally being accomplished. The goals are finalized and submitted, and the group (and/or leader) breaths a collective sigh. There is a celebration of sorts, or at least an acknowledgment of the task, before everyone returns to work. Then, about nine to ten months later, the process repeats.

When people work remotely some or all the time, these tendencies are exacerbated. The more people work alone, the more insular their work and the shorter their time horizons become. Because of this, the focus becomes more intense on the daily activities and less on the bigger-picture goals.

The problem organizations face mirrors our problem with books on goals: the focus is all on *setting* the goals, when it should be on achieving them. If you identify in any way with the somewhat cynical scenario we just described, we have good news: you can change these tendencies—and when you do, your team will quickly get better and have more lasting results.

Now that we have shared our perspective, let's talk a bit about setting more effective goals in a remote environment, and let's spend some important time on how we can help those goals get achieved.

Setting Goals Remotely

Most everyone agrees that goals should be SMART; a clever mnemonic that authors like to use. While not everyone uses the same words to complete the memory device, here is what we use:

- Specific

- Measurable

- Actionable

- Realistic

- Time-driven

The reason the mnemonic has become ubiquitous is that it is hard to argue with the wisdom of the five attributes: when those attributes are true about a goal statement, you have improved the chances that the goal will be reached.

In our experience, people find two of these criteria the hardest to master and the most difficult to make work from a distance: making them measurable and determining what realistic looks like. Let's talk about these two and identify the nuances of these challenges when you are not always working in the same location.

Making Them Measurable

Some goals are easy to measure—if you are leading a sales team (remotely or otherwise), it is pretty simple because a sales goal is clearly measurable. Look at the sales numbers and you will know where you are and how close you are to the goal. For many other roles you don't have to think too hard to find measurable targets. But with some jobs, there may not be an obvious financial or tangible target and you might have to work harder to create measurable goals.

To make the work of others more measurable, ask how else you can quantify their effort and contributions. These questions might help:

- What are the *quantity* components of the work?

- How does *time* factor into the success of the work?

- How is the *quality* of the work determined?

Remember, although we have tried to dispel the worries you might have about what people are doing when you can't see them working every day, when you can find measurable targets, your concerns in this area should be further reduced. While measurements should always be clear, when working with team members who are remote, setting measures in smaller chunks can be even more important. When people work alone, in their own bubble, and the targets are too big, it is easy for them to let too much time pass before they realize they need to course correct. Maybe they're struggling with a challenge but don't want to admit they're having trouble. Or perhaps they are working under assumptions that are no longer true—they literally missed the memo.

Wayne calls these Wile E. Coyote moments. In the classic *Road Runner* cartoons, Wile E. Coyote is often in such hot pursuit of his target (the Road Runner) that he runs off the edge of the cliff. We laugh in the pause before he falls to the canyon floor, but it isn't a laughing matter to him. Nor will it be to your team members when they realize they've gone too far and need to start over, do a bunch of rework, or make major adjustments. Measuring progress frequently, and with intent, makes a difference. If you can see that Margaret is on track, you can relax. If you know that Bob is nearing a deadline, you might want to ask if he needs added resources or help with anything.

While these questions certainly help, they don't solve the challenge of making goals measurable for all jobs, or all parts of every job.

Think about Frank, our sales manager. Certainly, he's measuring how many outbound calls or appointments his reps do. But is he checking on how often they've talked to their peers? If sharing of best practices is a goal at the team level, has his top producer contributed to the Q&A site, or helped a newbie since Frank asked him to?

Two Types of Goals

We've already talked about the *what* and the *how* of people's work. Most people think about goals in terms of what (or results)—which we have just discussed. But that doesn't always cut it, or it doesn't give a full picture of *how* people are doing (process goals). If you are still a bit worried about how to know what your folks are doing when they aren't working in the office, these types of goals can help you tremendously.

Jeffrey and Jami Downs expanded on an important strategy in their book *Streaking: The Simple Practice of Conscious, Consistent Actions That Create Life-Changing Results*. The idea is simple: translate your results goal into a process action that you can repeat. If your goal is to run a marathon, you can create a "streak" of daily runs. Each day you run, you put an X on your calendar. Your goal is to not break the streak of Xs.

We can attest to this strategy working (though not with marathons for either of us), and once you think about it, you can see it in many places:

- There are a bevy of habit apps that fundamentally provide this calendar.

- This type of activity measure is a key tool in *gamification*—making activities and learning more like playing a game.

- The correlation between this strategy and addiction-cessation groups (AA, NA, etc.) is clear.

Maybe the X is on an online dashboard (tools like Microsoft SharePoint, your intranet, or your project management software), where you and your remote team members can easily access and see it. Maybe progress is reported weekly, to both the employee and the leader, or maybe you discuss it in your ongoing one-on-ones (more on these later). Whether shared widely or not, the streak helps maintain focus, motivation, and accountability. Use your circumstances, the nature of the work, and work with your team to determine what your process goals might be. The result will be helpful, motivating, and lead to more measurable goals.

What about Realistic?

The other question we hear about SMART goals is "How do you know it is realistic?" Here is what it shouldn't mean:

- It isn't obvious that it will be reached.

- It isn't so big that people don't believe it is even possible.

A realistic goal is one that stretches our belief, yet we can create a workable real-world plan that might allow us to reach it.

Think of a rubber band and the tension it can provide. If we let the rubber band lie limp on the desk, it doesn't help us in any way. This is analogous to the obvious goal. When we pull it past the breaking point, the band is of no value to us either—this is like the target that is so big that it doesn't help us; in fact, it demotivates us. But when we stretch the rubber band just a bit, the tension begs us to move in the direction of the stretch. This is our metaphor for powerful, helpful, realistic targets and why setting and achieving goals at the right level is so important.

Like Goldilocks and her porridge, too cold and too hot aren't great; you want it just right.

We wish we could give you a specific and solid definition or answer to the "What is realistic anyway?" or "What is just right?" questions, but like all good consultants, we'll start by saying, "it depends."

What does *realistic* depend on?

- *Past performance.* If last year, your team member completed four process-improvement projects, five or six might be realistic, but ten might not be. If you have a team member that did nine last year, ten seems like a slam-dunk, and maybe thirteen or fourteen is a better target.

- *Level of confidence.* Confidence plays a role in our achievement; if you have a team member whose confidence in general or on this task is low, you will want to take that into account when setting a realistic goal. This isn't an excuse for low performance, but it is part of your role as a leader to help them build their confidence so that they can achieve at higher levels.

- *Recent development or skill trajectory.* How are people building their skills? If they have done far better in the last quarter than in the previous three, perhaps the annual goal is based on the more recent performance, not the full year.

- *Outlook on the world.* Related to confidence, the cynics or Eeyores of the world will feel like the goals need to be lower too—they see the obstacles, pitfalls, and potential negatives easily. This is a coaching opportunity, yet you must remember that people's personal beliefs will impact what they see as realistic.

Look at this list again and you will see that except for past performance, all of these can be harder for us to see or recognize at a distance. If your team members are only in the office sporadically or you rarely see them, you won't notice these factors unless you are regularly meeting with them and intentionally looking at/listening to/observing their communication and interaction.

Making Them Realistic

Here are some suggestions to make the goals of your remote team members more realistic (this is a good overall process for setting them collaboratively too—it just happens to help create realistic targets at the same time):

- *Provide the needed information.* Make sure everyone knows what this year's performance goals are, what the organizational targets for next year are, and the relative importance and priority of the goal being set.

- *Expect engagement.* Let people know (especially if this is a new idea for them) that the goal-setting process will be collaborative. Ask them to come to the discussion prepared and that you expect that preparation to be more than a thought as they turn on their webcam. Make sure they know whether they need to turn the webcam on; without the visual information, you can't see the worried look on their face or their shoulders slump in despair. Remember, there's a big difference between compliance and buy-in.

- *Get their thoughts first.* If you want realistic goals that people will be committed to, you must create a conversation. As the boss, you won't have a conversation if you start talking first, or if you dominate the conversation. If your team members aren't prepared with their thoughts about the goals, it's better to reschedule after reiterating the expected outcome and your desire for them to be prepared rather than plowing forward with your ideas first. Be careful that you set aside enough time for this meeting, as it's more common to worry about wasting time in a virtual environment than it is when you're sitting together over a cup of coffee. Not only does your time together need to be a priority, the employees, needs prove that it's important.

- *Modify with your thoughts, if needed.* If we want team members to have ownership of the goals, the goals need to be theirs. But if they set targets that you see as too easy or not quite in alignment with the organizational needs, you may need to help them stretch the rubber band. Don't just unilaterally change the target, talk about it; help them see that a bigger target can be realistic to both of you. Ensure that the conversation raises their comfort level and confidence in reaching that raised target. Just because you want agreement doesn't mean you have to acquiesce to the target they pick—you are the leader, after all.

- *Gain agreement.* Once you have SMART goals that everyone can live with, you have your best chance of hitting those goals. If you work toward true agreement, you might only get to understanding or compliance, but even then, the conversation is worth the time.

So far, we've been talking about individual goals, but the same rules apply to group objectives. Whether you have the whole team together for this conversation or you are using your web-conference tools, the process is the same. Kevin uses this basic approach in setting the company's revenue targets each year. If the goal is to have team ownership of the targets, it must begin with people having the information they need and with them creating a conversation about the targets. If he provides the targets as the boss and then asks, "What do you think?" He'll likely get one of two responses:

- Disagreement, with no clear way to move forward.

- Acquiescence, where people tacitly agree, but never really own the target or have much sense of how realistic it is. Again, compliance is not ownership, and when you're not in the room, you miss a lot of the visual and nonverbal cues that will tell you which you're getting.

Making the goals or targets realistic is important; you will know the goals are realistic when they provide your team with guidance and motivation, and when you and your team agree on them.

Plan for Achievement Early

We've said that, too often, the focus (organizationally and personally) is on setting goals and not on achieving them. The easiest and most tangible way to overcome this common problem is to link the goal setting and goal planning processes together.

We have found that even for leaders and organizations that agree with this point, this is an area of collaboration that has been sacrificed as people work at a distance. We suggest you reinforce the value of coupling goal setting and achievement together and make it a higher priority.

Energy, enthusiasm, and goal clarity are often highest when goals are first set. Take advantage of this by spending time planning for goal achievement as soon as possible after setting the goals.

If you create the goals collaboratively, you might not want to go forward with planning immediately, although a chance to think about the goals for a bit or sleep on them can be very helpful. But close the goal-setting meeting by deciding when you will finish the planning. Get it on the calendar and decide what technology to use for this important work. As long as the plan is created within a few days, you will capitalize on most of these "early-mover" benefits.

Reaching Goals Remotely

Even if you plan goal achievement steps as quickly as you can after setting the goals, that isn't the full story. You must do the work and execute the plan. Remember—if reaching goals was easy, there wouldn't be so many books written on the topic.

Goals aren't achieved in a vacuum. Priorities shift, emergencies arise, and stuff happens. When all of that occurs remotely, it is even harder to recognize, offer assistance, and change gears. Often employees make decisions on their own that impact their long-term goals and those of the team, and you won't know until it's too late. As a Long-Distance Leader you and your people need to have a process that allows for the unexpected while keeping everyone on the same track. Here's our advice:

Set clear expectations upfront.

Once you have a plan, make sure everyone is clear that the plan isn't a suggestion, it's a roadmap. Even a GPS recalculates but keeps you headed toward your goal. Make sure both you and the team members understand the plan, have thought through how it will work in the realities of daily work, and know what to do when the unexpected arises.

Visualize the outcome.

In 1971 when Disney World opened, Roy Disney (Walt's brother and a company executive) was asked what Walt would have thought if he could have seen it completed (Walt died during construction). Roy's short answer: "You don't understand. Walt already saw it. That is why we are here." When we take time to help people literally see the result in three dimensions, the goal will more likely be reached. Tap into this 3D picture in conversations with people, especially when the challenges mount and they are frustrated by a lack of progress. If people work in-office some days, schedule these conversations in person if possible. If people are fully remote, use your meeting tools and webcams to make the conversations as rich and effective as possible.

Expect consistent implementation.

The best way to reach a goal is by working on it regularly. Encourage your team members to consistently work on their goal achievement plan. Individual steps don't have to be big; it's progress that matters—regular small advances typically outpace the occasional effort. Make progress on goal plans a regular part of your conversations and one-on-ones. This communication keeps you in the loop, helps you remove barriers quickly, and reinforces the importance of reaching the goal. This will reduce stress on both parties—as the leader you are getting the information you need, but because it has been mutually agreed to, your team member likely won't see you as micromanaging them.

Provide time.

If the goals are important enough to set, time must be provided to work on them. As leaders, we must help people manage their time and allow enough discretionary time for goal work to happen. Remember that when people work remotely, they may solve this problem by working more hours, or by unintentionally neglecting tasks that others rely on. Help them be successful by carefully analyzing their workload and scheduling time to work on these goals.

Protect the time.

Working on goals is important. We'll bet you have scheduled important work on your calendar before but have had it slip away when a meeting came up or when the urgent items of the day melted that scheduled time away.

While we wouldn't wish this hypothetical on anyone, imagine this scenario for a second. If you had previously experienced some heart problems and you had a scheduled appointment with your cardiologist, would you cancel it for the same kinds of reasons you cancel other appointments you might take? Probably not. So, when you (or your team members) schedule time to work on something important—like goal achievement or an important project—allow that time to be sacred, like cardiologist time.

When your remote team members are comfortable enough to schedule this kind of time and when they have a way to block time off and communicate it to others so that they will not be disturbed, your whole team will achieve more goals faster than you imagined. For this process to work best as a remote or hybrid team, team members must share their calendars and have a forum for discussing deadlines and priorities. And, if a person is working on heads-down goals work, everyone needs to leave them alone—even their boss.

Make them a priority.

If the only time goals are a priority is when you set them, you haven't much chance of achieving them, and perhaps you'd have been better off not setting them at all. If you are doing the other things on this list, like prioritizing and protecting time, your team members will also see the goals as a priority.

Report and discuss regularly.

One of the best things you can do to help people achieve their goals is to talk about them regularly. This means real conversation, not just "reporting out."

Progress reports or status updates are great, but they may not allow people to share a concern or for you to see if they are overly confident. If you want to achieve more, make goal progress a regular part of your conversations. Setting smaller, incremental targets creates reasons to connect more frequently. If you won't bump into each other in the hallway, you need to be more intentional about creating these short but critical interactions.

Provide resources.

Part of your job as leader is to help people remove the barriers and give them the tools and resources to make their plans happen. Time is one resource, but there may be others, like letting them know who else in the organization they can rely on for information or expertise. Do your job—help them reach the goals that have been set.

Be flexible.

One of the biggest complaints we hear about goal setting in organizations is that the world is changing so fast that setting goals isn't productive. There is truth here—mergers happen, new projects arrive, new products are developed, and priorities shift. We need to be flexible with the goals and their priority and be willing to move some to the back burner (or remove them from the list entirely). Our advice here is three-fold:

- Acknowledge that things might change as the year goes on.

- Work together to make the required adjustments.

- Continue to make goals a critical part of your work.

Pause and Reflect

Ask yourself these questions:

▶ Are my goals SMART?

▶ Have I considered process-oriented goals as well as results-oriented ones?

▶ Am I using (enough of) them?

▶ Am I placing too much focus on setting the goals . . . and in effect not spending enough focus on the plan for achieving them?

▶ How can I help my team reach the goals that have been set?

Online Resources

If you would like more help and ideas, go to KevinEikeberry.com for a complete list of our services, thought leadership, and free resources.

To identify the biggest skill and knowledge gaps in your organization directly related to working remotely, register at LongDistanceWorklife.com/Resources and request the Remote Goal Setting Checklist Tool.

Chapter 8

Coaching and Feedback at a Distance

Rule 8: Coach your team effectively regardless of where and how they work.

One of the best things you can do for other people is to help them recognize how they can improve.

—Wess Roberts, author

Helen is struggling with her customer service team. Half are in the call center, the rest work from home. She knows that coaching and ongoing feedback are critical to the success of her team, and she's always tried to be an effective coach. Recent feedback, though, shows that the people she is co-located with are much happier with her coaching efforts than her remote folks. She's struggling to schedule time with those who work from home, and the coaching sessions are much less satisfying for both her and the employees. She's wondering what she is doing wrong or needs to change.

Coaching in general is a broad topic, and entire books and curricula are built around the subject. At the beginning of this book, we made some assumptions—that you are already familiar with most of the basics of leadership, including the need for coaching, and that you are willing to coach your people. If your organization has a prescribed model or process for coaching, what follows will augment those efforts well. If you don't already have a prescribed method for coaching, we suggest the simple model outlined in Kevin's book *Remarkable Leadership*.

The Remote Difference

If we were to pick a big area of leadership competence that needs improvement, it would be coaching. Working remotely creates an additional layer of complexity to the part of the job in which we're already least secure. The fundamentals of coaching—having clear expectations and goals, building a relationship, providing both encouragement and correction—don't change whether you're in the same room or an ocean apart, but somehow it seems harder the farther away you are.

There are two big reasons coaching remotely feels more complicated and stressful:

Every interaction needs to be conscious and intentional.   When you aren't working in the same location, you don't run into people in the breakroom or catch sight of them out of the corner of your eye and wander over to their cubicle for a quick chat. When they are remote, you need to intentionally get their attention and take time out of whatever else you (and they) are working on. If you're the kind of person who's tempted to avoid these types of conversations anyway, less (and less effective) coaching is the result.

Communicating through technology creates mental and social obstacles that don't exist in person.   We naturally communicate best when we are physically in the presence of other people. When we are remote, we are working through technology that, even though we use it all the time, may feel like a barrier. Being "on Zoom" also tends to make conversations more transactional and rushed. If you've ever caught yourself beginning an online conversation with "this will only take a minute and then you can get back to work" and then rushing through what should have been a meatier discussion, you know what we mean.

The Benefit of Hybrid

If you have hybrid team members, the good news is that while you can provide coaching at a distance, you don't always have to. Make sure you use the time when you are in person to coach and have in-depth conversations. This point is critical—prioritize the work that is most beneficial in person when you are in person!

Important Basics

What follows is true about all coaching, but doing these things well is especially important if we are to address the two issues we just described.

Keep accountability clear.

Great coaches care and think about the performance and skills of their team members. As a leader, you feel responsible if someone doesn't perform well. You may think about what else you could have taught them, another way you could have inspired them, or any number of other things. Although it is important to think about what else you could have done, in the end, the final accountability for performance lies with the performer. Your job is to promote their confidence, skill, and proficiency but they are doing the work.

Check your beliefs.

Whatever you believe about your team member drastically affects their ability to be successful in their work. Think about it this way: if you believe someone can be successful, you look for the clues, examples, emails, and results that confirm your belief in them. But the opposite is also true. Once you have an opinion about someone, you've decided. And as true as that is when you work face to face with people every day, it is even more true when you don't see them as often. This is called *confirmation bias*, which is enhanced in a remote environment because we have less data to draw on. People are usually less aware of conflicting evidence because they don't process electronic information the same way they do in person. Because you often scan emails, unless something really jumps out at you, you're likely to miss subtle clues that don't fit your notions of that person's competence and motives.

Assume positive intent; be prepared to be wrong.

Consider the two basic assumptions we make about people's capabilities and the results they lead to:

- At the start of the coaching conversation, you assume the best—that people's intents were in the right place; that even if they messed up or fell short of a goal or deadline, there were plausible and understandable reasons.

- At the start of the coaching conversation, you assume the worst—that the person was either aware of the gap, but apparently didn't care, or they were in some way unaware of the problem.

Isn't it fair to say that your initial assumption will affect the way you ask questions and give feedback? We believe that starting from a place of positive intent will not only be more accurate most of the time but will get better coaching results.

Wayne says that this is one of Kevin's great strengths, but like any strength, it can become a weakness, which is why we added "be prepared to be wrong." You can assume positive intent and be wrong. And when you are, you need to coach from a more stern and clear position. These conversations may not be easy, especially remotely, but by using the lessons we share throughout the book, we believe you can succeed.

Remember that coaching isn't about where people are today but where they can be. You must look for reasons to believe in others and their potential. If you don't start with the belief that people are coachable, you won't do it. If they are remote, you will have to try harder and be more intentional. When people work in a hybrid model, you need to focus on them more and be more observant when you are physically present with them. Doing these things is worth the effort.

Make sure it is a true, real conversation.

Too many coaches do too much of the talking too much of the time. If you want to be a better coach, create a real, two-way conversation with the other person about their behavior and results. The best way to create a conversation is by letting them speak first, so start by asking them questions. When you're doing this remotely, make the conversation as effective as possible (this is one time to turn on the webcams) and even send the question you have in advance so the person is prepared for the conversation. When there is a pause in the conversation, end the silence with a question, not a statement. It's easy to fall into the trap of doing too much of the talking, especially if you are on the phone and can't gauge how the other person is reacting. Remember that if you talk to end a silence, you are teaching others to be quiet and let you talk. If you are doing all the talking, their ownership is likely diminishing sentence by sentence. This is especially true because you are the boss ("the boss is talking, so I better let them talk"). The natural power differential isn't helping you here. Do everything you can to strike a balance. Ask more first, and talk less.

Make sure the job expectations are crystal clear.

As we saw in our 3O Model, first and foremost, leaders must coach toward achieving outcomes. While clear expectations don't guarantee success, effective coaching and great outcomes hinge on clear expectations. If people aren't clear on the expectations, this becomes job one in the coaching process. One of the best ways to make the expectations clear is to write them down. We believe that providing them in writing may actually be easier with a remote team member. If you just use the phone, you may naturally wonder if the other person is writing things down or is even listening. When you are using technology to have the coaching conversation, the notes and documented expectations can be visible to both of you as you collaborate on a shared screen. This makes for easier reference and clarity during and after the conversation and increases the odds of your team member gaining the needed clarity. You're literally seeing things the same way at the same time.

Have a process.

As we have already said, if you have a coaching process, use it. Most coaching models are built assuming face-to-face communication, but if you stop and consider all the ideas in this book (including the chapters to come on communication and technology use), you'll be fine. While team members don't need to know the model or approach you are using, they'll benefit from the consistency that the approach creates in the way you coach. You reduce the angst and uncertainty others will have when they know more about how, and how often, you will coach.

Make coaching consistent and frequent.

We can't say this enough: people need (and when it is done well, want) ongoing coaching and feedback. Think about it this way: if you do something well but never get any feedback, you might unknowingly change how you do the process and make it worse or less effective, or at a minimum, keep trying new approaches with varying success. If you get some feedback that you are on the right track, you will lock in that behavior and start to create an effective habit. Alternatively, if you are doing something wrong, and you aren't aware, you may keep doing it, assuming it is fine, and build a habit of doing it wrong. Both situations can be avoided if your leader provides you with ongoing feedback.

Have a recurring timeline for formal, scheduled coaching. When your team is working remotely you will be tempted to make these conversations shorter and more infrequent. Don't give in to this temptation! This is critical time and should be a priority. There will also be informal coaching moments, which we'll talk about shortly.

Use your webcam.

Coaching is important enough to make the communication as effective as possible. Why do we think face to face is better than using the phone? Because we rely on visual and nonverbal cues to help us communicate. Our brains crave visual connection to the people we speak with. Webcams, and other tools we'll discuss in the next part, help mitigate the fact that you're not in the same room with the person you're talking to.

If you meet with reluctant webcamers, it is okay to not force them to use the cam all the time—they will appreciate that acknowledgment and flexibility. Just know that if you only ask them to use the webcam for what you perceive as the tough conversation, you have a new problem of raising their stress before the conversation even begins! Be flexible, but request/insist on using the cam some of the time so that when you're using it, it doesn't always mean that you're having a "big deal" conversation.

Follow up.

Too often, a leader and team member have a coaching conversation, they determine a plan of action to help people move forward, and then . . . nothing. The follow-up might not happen because of poor time management, or a lack of discipline, or simply because someone assumes the best and lets things slip through the cracks. Your team will treat the coaching or the gap in performance as if it wasn't *that* important. In the worst case, a cynical team member might not love the once-a-quarter conversation about their reports being late, but it is easier to endure an occasional conversation than change their behavior; without follow-up, *your* behavior tells them it isn't *that* important. And as frequently as coaches of teams down-the-hall mess this up, remote leaders are often worse. Sometimes, Helen, the Customer Service manager, would get off the phone and then remember she wanted to talk to a team member about something, but the opportunity had passed. Or the call happened while she was in transit and so she needed to keep it as short as possible, which was not ideal for the kind of conversations we're talking about. At least when you're working together, you can see someone in the hallway or pass by their desk, and that may prompt you to speak to that person. When people aren't seen, you can't rely on spontaneity; you must be focused and intentional about all your follow-up.

Check in, don't check up.

We love this phrase because even the most confident, skilled team members will be fine (and usually appreciate) when you check in with them on how things are going, especially if these check-ins are regular and expected. Even the least-seasoned person who may not be performing very well doesn't like to be "checked up on." The difference between the two is often perception. First, make sure that your intention is to support and help by checking in, not by figuratively looking over the person's shoulder. The best way to manage this perception is to plan in advance how you can help; let them know when and how you will be available, and gain agreement on how, and how often, you'll communicate when setting your goals and expectations. By reaching agreement on the frequency of these check-in points early, you improve the chances that your intention won't be misread.

You must coach, even when it's uncomfortable.

Coaching is part of a leader's job, but at a distance, it can be tempting to take the easy way out when it gets hard. You have a team member who is doing something poorly or making an error. Maybe it isn't a big problem, but it still needs to be addressed. You put it off and secretly hope it will get better, or you just don't like confrontation, so you send an email instead of having a conversation. Some leaders use time zones as the excuse to avoid addressing a problem as proactively as they should. By ignoring, procrastinating, or avoiding the need for the coaching, you are giving tacit approval, and the behavior will continue. Just because you don't see someone in the hallway several times a day doesn't mean you can take the easy way out and avoid providing the coaching they need so they can succeed. Doing this isn't fair to anyone, especially the remote team member. If you are coaching the people you see differently (or more often), you may unintentionally create the perception of favoritism. That's corrosive to team morale and employee engagement.

Giving Feedback

Feedback isn't coaching, but almost all coaching includes feedback. Here are six common questions about feedback and ways to address the nuances at a distance.

How is feedback accepted?

Try as we might to give feedback in the best way, at the best time, and with the best words, how our feedback is received starts with the other person's perception. The other person decides how to take a leader's input, and its value, based on three factors:

- *Position.* If you are the boss, you have some positional power and so people will likely listen to your feedback but not necessarily value it as highly as you might like. This factor is the one you have automatically, but it is the least valuable of the three. Are you relying solely on this? If so, you're likely only getting compliance.

- *Expertise.* People value feedback from people they view as knowing what they are talking about. If your team members don't recognize your experience with or knowledge of what you are giving feedback on, it will be less valued. And as a Long-Distance Leader, it may be harder for you to establish that credibility. Make it your goal for people to know your background to establish this credibility, but do so without being arrogant or cocky. Make it clear that you want to understand their working situation too—especially if you are in-office and they are mostly (or fully) remote. Remember that you don't have all the expertise. Maybe some feedback would be more effective coming from someone on the team who has the expertise.

- *Relationship.* We have all asked people for feedback about a situation they know little about. Why? Because we trust them and their intentions. We know that they will be honest and that their feedback is meant to help us, even if it is hard to hear. As a Long-Distance Leader, it will take more effort to build strong relationships with your team members; it's worth the effort.

What do we give feedback on?

We must give feedback on the things that matter—on the parts of the job that are most important, that make the biggest impact, and that can create the most valuable results. Chances are you've been given feedback on something that seemed insignificant and petty. It's a good bet that you didn't feel great about that feedback, or about the person who delivered it to you—and it gets worse in a remote relationship where there is less overall interaction. Make sure you deliver feedback on what is meaningful, not just on what you can see, and if it is meaningful, make sure people see why.

What makes it helpful?

Feedback is helpful when it's clear and specific. The best ways to make sure those things are true is to use examples; have evidence and give the feedback based on observable behavior. If you have clear data, it reduces the length of time and strength of people's defensiveness and increases the chance for acceptance. Use technology to share screens so both you and the person receiving your feedback can see the relevant data. "Avoid telling the customer they were wrong" is more specific than "You need to be more careful about what you put in your email." In some situations, making it observable might be harder if you haven't actually seen the behavior yourself. Harder, but not impossible. Make collecting data and observations (and capturing them to share at the right time) an intentional part of your daily work. And remember, making it clear, and specific, with examples isn't just for the things that are going wrong. The same criteria apply when people do well, which leads us to the next question.

What about the balance of positive to negative feedback?

We believe, and the research backs us up, that most people don't receive enough positive feedback in the workplace; from their boss or anyone else. This is even more true when people work remotely or in a hybrid environment. The more time people spend in the office with their boss, the happier they are with the feedback they get. When giving feedback over the phone or virtually, the tendency is for the feedback to become more transactional. Given that, it's likely that the "necessary" negative or corrective feedback will be shared more than the positive, encouraging input. Real, positive feedback is just as critical, and we must remember to share it. Keep a list of things— positive and corrective—for each team member that you can refer to in your one-on-ones or informal moments (whether in person or virtually). And don't just toss in some fluffy positives just so you can feel like you are giving balanced feedback. People need to know and will grow when they know both what they are doing well and what they need to adjust. Since they are likely doing some of each, it is our job to make sure we notice and share a balanced view of what is going on.

How to deliver it?

If you are going to provide feedback, you should be prepared. Take the time to collect your thoughts, have examples, and be clear on what you want to share (and when you have been writing things down, this will be easier and far more effective). Unfortunately, when we *are* well prepared, our first inclination is to start the conversation by sharing what we have prepared. Instead, open by asking the person to share feedback on themselves. Questions like: "How is it going from your perspective?" or "What feedback would you give yourself?" are good ways to create a conversation. If you, as the boss, go first, what is really left for them to share? If you are doing this over the phone, remember that pauses seem longer and even more uncomfortable, so you may start talking too soon. If having the conversation with the webcam, also be ready to be more patient. You want their input, so be patient and wait for it.

Are you looking forward?

Most feedback is given on what has already happened—perhaps that is why it is called feed*back*. Feedback about the past is helpful and provides context and data, but for this information to be helpful, it needs to be about what comes next. Marshall Goldsmith calls this feed*forward*—commentary about what the person should do or change *in the future*.[1] Again, when we are coaching and providing feedback at a distance, the risk is that we don't take ample time to make the feedback complete, and we don't connect the dots for people to show them how what has passed can inform what happens next time or confirm true understanding.

What about Performance Management?

Performance management and performance reviews matter to all your team members, regardless of where they work. As with other facets of leading at a distance, you must be more conscious, intentional, and focused on your team members to do this well.

For your remote team members, we find that the intentionality needed to think longer and think differently is difficult. Since their interactions with their remote folks are more infrequent, leaders tend to focus on the tasks—including filling out the performance appraisal form. By now you know the problems with that approach.

We have created an online tool to assist you in doing this well. Go to LongDistanceWorklife.com/Perfmanagement.

Getting Delegation Right

Delegation has confounded leaders for a long time. We believe the problem is less about the steps of doing the delegating because once you have decided, for the right reasons, to delegate, it is all about teaching and coaching. If we approach delegation correctly, doing it at a distance just requires some adjustments.

What We All Say about Delegation

Nearly everyone can complete two phrases in unison in our workshops when talking about delegation:

- "If you want something done right, you should _____."

- "It would take longer to delegate (or teach someone) than it would to just _____."

In case you aren't tracking, the answers are "do it yourself."

These two statements are often used as an excuse for not delegating, and both statements are true *at this moment*. If you are thinking about delegating something you have done yourself many times, you *will* do it better and faster than a first-timer. But delegation isn't about the first time, it is about the long term, and it's not about you, it's about helping the individual achieve the organization's goals (notice the 3O Model—the focus on both Outcomes and Others). If you want people to succeed in doing a new task, you must think of delegation as an investment of time—both yours and theirs.

Delegating takes patience, time, and effort. It will likely take restraint on your part (not to step in and do what you are trying to delegate), and it will likely be even harder when you're delegating at a distance. Take more time up front, set a plan for check-in conversations (which will look different depending on what is being delegated, but the point of check-ins is important), and focus on the other person's success rather than on getting rid of the task yourself.

The Focus

Lots of leadership books tell you that as a leader you must delegate. Your time is precious and if you don't delegate, your plate will be overflowing and you will have no work/life balance. While we agree with the point, we believe there is an unintended consequence in that line of thinking: that delegation is something you need to do for yourself.

That is the wrong focus.

If you delegate for solely selfish reasons—just to get the task off your list, for example—you will likely go about it wrong, with too little patience, and you will likely "prove" the statements we made earlier. In other words, as Kevin says, you won't be delegating, you will be dumping work on someone.

When you realize that delegation is about helping someone else succeed at a new task and grow in their responsibilities and contribution to the team, and that delegation will take some time and be worth that investment, you will likely go about it just fine. The person you are delegating to will likely accept the work and succeed at it, and you will have created a more flexible team in the process.

When giving feedback virtually, the tendency is for the feedback to become more transactional.

And when you do all that, you will lessen your load a bit too, which is also important.

Stated another way, when you keep the 3O Model in mind, by placing yourself last, delegation will work better, and you will get all the benefits you wanted too.

There are two additional wrinkles to delegation in a remote or hybrid team environment. One is reality-based and the other is a matter of perception—and one contributes to the other. *Proximity bias* is when we tend to show favoritism or preferential treatment to those we can see or to those who are in the same location. This isn't new but has become a much bigger concern as more people work in the office part time or not at all.

Let's say you have a project you need to delegate or use as a development opportunity. Proximity bias says you will most likely hand it to someone you can see or who is nearby. While this bias applies to more issues than just delegation, here is a perfect place to talk about it. The perception may be reality—the people in-office (or who are there the same days you are) get the plum projects and the less-than-glamorous stuff too. The people who are remote don't feel seen or that they are being given the chance to develop. The in-office people feel they get dumped on. Whether reality or not, the perception of inequity and lack of inclusion is as corrosive as if you actually meant to treat people differently.

Proximity bias is real, and since it is a bias, you might be blind to it. Don't simply pass this off as a nonissue. You must do everything you can to create equality and inclusion. Are you?

Make sure that everyone on your team is aware of what the others are doing, and when a task is assigned, to whom. The perception of fairness is at least as important as actually being fair.

Great (Remote) One-on-One Coaching Meetings

The heart of the coaching process is the one-on-one meeting. This is a planned time to sit down and talk to your team member about how things are going and how you can help.

Many people think about the one-on-one as a status or update meeting and we agree that this is an important reason to meet (though often not in the same physical location). We also believe that these planned conversations can and should include a coaching component. To make your remote one-on-ones most effective, keep the following points in mind.

Have a schedule.

Talk with each team member to decide how often you will meet. If you feel you need to meet more frequently than they want, negotiate, or start with their preferred frequency while agreeing to adjust the timing in the future if you need to. If people work in a hybrid fashion, schedule these meetings on days you are together. Currently Kevin has six team members reporting to him. The frequency of one-on-ones isn't the same for each person. Factors like the nature of their work, their experience and confidence with the work, the type of support he can provide, and the personal preferences of the individual team members all play into the frequency of these meetings. In our experience, this frequency could be daily (though then there may be less coaching in each meeting) up to monthly. We typically recommend scheduling them somewhere between weekly and monthly based on the factors just described. Everything else being equal, we recommend greater frequency when people are remote. The one-on-one meeting is an important way to keep remote people connected because in so many ways, they aren't.

Use your tools.

Since you are having these one-on-ones, but they aren't face to face, we recommend making as many of them as you can as rich as possible. In other words, use webcams, screen sharing, and dashboard tools whenever applicable! As we travel we have witnessed too many important calls being made in airports or hotel lobbies (or even public restrooms). These meetings are important and shouldn't be crammed into a small opening on the calendar, or into time when one of you should be concentrating on something else, like driving to a client meeting. These one-on-ones, especially coaching conversations, need to take place when both parties can focus on the important topic of mutual success.

Create co-ownership of the meeting.

These meetings benefit both you and your team member. You want to be updated and have a chance to support, encourage, and correct people as needed, and they need direction, information, and encouragement. The meeting isn't yours or theirs—it must be owned by both of you. This means that both parties need to take these meetings seriously, come prepared, clear their calendars, and hold the other accountable for all of this. If you need to make this more obvious to your team member, keep a shared document into which you can both put items for discussion—use this document as the agenda for the meeting.

Let them go first.

The inherent power imbalance that exists because you are the boss means you must ensure mutual ownership of the meeting is maintained. Remember what we said earlier about letting the other person open the conversation. Kevin has messed this up many times in the past; now he has trained himself (he thinks) to stop and flip the conversation back to the other person if he starts off. Everyone wins when they go first. It is easier to forget this when you're more concerned about time or getting tasks done than why you are meeting in the first place.

Schedule whether to meet in person or online.

When your work situation allows, make time for face-to-face conversations. As we said, if people are only in the office two days a week, meet on those days. If people work farther away, use your in-person time wisely. Build relationships then, even if it means staying an extra day or catching a later flight (or having them do the same) to build connection, and use this added time to have the one-on-one you would normally have at a distance. Take advantage of face time whenever you can.

Informal Coaching When Remote

There is more to coaching than the planned one-on-one meeting. While less serendipitous in a remote work environment, the best leaders/coaches are always watching for opportunities to engage a team member, ask a question, or provide some encouragement or correction. Kevin often uses time at the end of a team call to engage one or two team members in quick conversations, one after the other, much as you might do after an in-person meeting in the conference room. By recognizing that opportunity, and by making it more casual in nature, he is creating these opportunities that would have otherwise been missed. Kevin does this intentionally and you can too—but you must plan and build that extra time into your calendar.

Because these informal moments are so important to performance and in creating ongoing feedback, we need to find ways to coach in informal ways and spontaneous situations better; or, said in a different way, we must find time to coach when we don't have time to coach.

The Informal Coaching Moment

The informal coaching moment isn't scheduled, preplanned, or on anyone's calendar. It's what Thomas Peters and Robert Waterman famously called "management by walking around" in their bestselling book *In Search of Excellence*.[2] When you are in close proximity to a person, pass them in the hall, walk past their desk, or when they poke their head into your office, you have the opportunity for the informal coaching moment. Such moments can include talking about what's going on, what's coming up for them, and how you can help.

For your remote team members, it's a long walk to where they are, but the point is the same. You must create ways to engage with your folks even though you don't see them all the time. You can do this with phone-call check-ins, a morning text or instant message, or in any other way in which you can let them know you are around, available, and accessible. This works in both directions. Wayne sends Kevin a quick Slack message almost every morning with a greeting and an opening for informal conversation. Kevin has learned to do the same with other remote team members (both those he leads and those he doesn't) because it works so well with Wayne. Doing that is the same (regardless of who instigates it) as the hello in the breakroom, or popping your head in the office door on the way to your desk. Most days there's nothing to report, but occasionally this routine provides a moment for a quick one-on-one or a chance for either person to ask or answer a question. The additional benefit of this habit is that it can be a cultural clue—it shows team members it is okay to do that with others, not just with the boss.

Preparing for the Moment

While you can (and should) be intentional about creating these moments to check in and provide encouragement and guidance, they shouldn't feel contrived or forced. If you have questions about the business, the team member's results or project progress, or anything else, make a list. That list might be mental or (better) documented. Be prepared, but be prepared to really engage and connect, not to grill the person or drill down to specific points the moment you get together.

Creating the Moment

If you have team members onsite, you may say hello, ask them about their hobby, weekend, or family, and then use open-ended questions to shift gears from relationship building to a business check-in and a coaching moment. When they are working remotely, use the call, text, or instant message as the way to open the door. Remember that a big part of the success of informal coaching meetings is engaging with the other person. Start by getting them to talk about what is happening, how they are doing, and how you can help (the components of an informal coaching moment). Here are some simple questions to start and continue the informal coaching moment:

- "What's up?"

- "How's it going?"

- "What's working?"

- "Where are you stuck?"

- "How can I help?"

These questions are short (only fifteen words in five questions!) and open-ended enough to allow the other person to point the conversation where they need it to go. Once the conversation is moving, you might redirect it with a more specific question in context, but that will depend on how the conversation develops.

Notice one of our examples wasn't "Do you have a minute?" Few things are more terrifying to someone working from home than an IM/text from the boss that simply asks, "Do you have a minute?" The goal isn't to catch people off guard or make them feel pressured or unprepared. If you lead with this question, by the time you get that person in conversation, they've already imagined every horrible scenario possible. Even if you just want to pass on good news, you may have just created unintentional stress. Wayne often asks, "Do you have a moment? Nothing important, just a question." That helps set a more positive tone and reduces everyone's blood pressure.

Keep Coaching Moments Short

For the most part, the informal coaching moment should be moments, not minutes, or a half hour, in length. If the conversation develops and you both need or want more time, of course you will mutually decide on how to move the conversation forward appropriately.

Helen, in our example, has transformed her relationships and the performance and results of her team members. None of this replaces or erases the need for more formal planned performance and coaching conversations and standing one-on-ones, as we have discussed, but when you leverage informal coaching moments, your meetings will be more productive, and likely less frequent.

Pause and Reflect

Ask yourself these questions:

▶ How successfully am I at coaching my remote team members? (Would they answer the same way?)

▶ Are my remote, hybrid, and fully onsite team members getting the same quality and frequency of feedback from me? (Have I asked them what they think?)

▶ How transparent am I with the full team when delegating tasks?

▶ How intentional am I in finding moments to connect with and coach my remote team members?

Online Resources

If you would like more help and ideas, go to KevinEikeberry.com for a complete list of our services, thought leadership, and free resources.

To identify the biggest skill and knowledge gaps in your organization directly related to working remotely, register at LongDistanceWorklife.com/Resources and request the Sample Coaching Model.

Part III Summary

So What?

- How successful am I at setting goals (at all levels) with my team?

- Would my team's answer to the previous question be the same as mine? (If not, you might want to think about this some more.)

- Which ideas in the areas of coaching and feedback could I implement to improve the results for me and my team?

- Am I meeting with my remote team members often enough and with the right preparation and intention?

Now What?

Other than spending time with these questions, here are some actions to take, based on the ideas we covered in this part.

- Review your goals and implementation plans personally, with each team member, and as a team.

- Have a conversation to see if people feel you are on track. If not, refocus on the goals and plans.

- Check your calendar. If it doesn't have any coaching on it this week, fix that right now.

- Find three positive, meaningful things to share with members of your team before the end of the day, then share them.

Part IV

Engaging Others

Leadership is the art of getting someone else to do
something you want done because he wants to do it.

—Dwight D. Eisenhower, 34th US President

Part IV Introduction

Employee engagement is the emotional commitment an
employee has to the organization and its goals.

—Kevin Kruse, author and speaker

As we discussed in the last part, understanding, translating, and communicating the goals of the organization is a critical part of the leadership job description. It's the outside ring of our 3O Model. Whether you want to be the best company in your niche or the most awarded Boy Scout troop in town, it all starts with understanding (and making sure everyone else understands) what needs to be done and why.

As hybrid work and remote work become the norm, engagement has become central to a leader's job. It is the primary reason for many return-to-office mandates. Attraction, recruitment, and retention of workers depends on how well an organization and its leaders can engage—and help their people choose to engage—with the work and each other.

To achieve these outcomes, you must engage your team members—including their hearts and minds. Engaging others at a distance is complicated and radically different than the ways we worked to engage people before.

In the old days, people might have worked hard because the boss was watching—the boss could pop in at any moment and find them doing something they shouldn't . . . or not doing what they should. *Leading remotely requires influence more than command.* Levels of accountability, trust, and proactive communication, while desirable in a traditional workplace, are absolutely critical when you're not in close physical proximity.

How you engage others in a digitally connected but physically isolated world will largely determine whether you hit your goals and how stressful it will be along the way.

Chapter 9

How Distance Changes Your Role

Rule 9: Leading remotely requires more awareness and intention.

Once trust is built, distance cannot kill it. Time and space
alone cannot destroy authentic connection.

—Vironika Tugaleva, author and digital nomad

Alisha is exhausted. Her team went fully remote during 2020 and remained that way for nearly two years. When many people around the company returned to the office, some of her team members balked and asked to keep working from home. As much as she supports the company's decision requiring her to be in the office as much as possible, she has found that the flexibility of working remotely allowed her more family time and less time wasted during the commute. She finds herself half-heartedly enforcing rules about coming into the office and putting in more aggregate hours because her days in the office are longer than before. The uncomfortable compromise that they call hybrid work has reduced turnover on her team, but it has added to her personal stress as she tries to accommodate everyone else's schedule. It doesn't feel sustainable.

Since the first edition of this book came out in 2018, we've gone through disease, social and political stress in many countries, and a sea change in how people view their work and their relationship to an employer. We've gone through a Great Resignation, a Great Reset, and many stressors and trends the business press has named. Getting back to our original workplaces wasn't as easy as pretending those events didn't happen.

This last point is important as we think about the future of work and assess our roles as leaders. Remember that Outcomes, Others, and Ourselves define our work. Two of those three have changed far more than the third.

The outcomes—the work you, your organization, and your team do—have probably largely remained the same. Customers need to be served, reports written, parts ordered. *What* we do hasn't changed, as we pointed out in the Remote Leadership Model. But *how* we work, and notably, how our people work with each other (and you) has changed.

Some of these changes are obvious; others are more subtle. People have had time to reexamine whether work needs to involve long commutes, living close to the office, and time away from the family. Some people may decide going back to the way things were isn't acceptable. The resulting objections to returning to the "Before Times" led to people negotiating how many days a week or a month they needed to be in the office or to quitting outright.

Few people saw the other changes coming. The way people behave when they come together has changed, and not necessarily for the better. Many of our clients report that the dress code has pretty much gone out the window. What was a business-dress environment is now business casual, at best, and many folks can't agree on what that means. The norms of office behavior, from where people sit during meetings to not stealing other's yogurt in the breakroom changed, causing conflict and confusion. As one client told us, "It's like people have gone feral and we have to retrain them in how we work around here."

Adding to all of this is a crop of new employees, hired during the lock-downs, who have never worked in person. There is no way they can know the norms from before.

To lead in the modern long-distance workplace is to recognize how working with others, and how we manage ourselves, requires self-awareness and intentionality.

Leading Others

Leading others, either in a fully remote or in a hybrid manner, requires us to make some adjustments to the model we follow for in-person work. How much we trust each other, how we coach our people, and how we hire and keep top talent are part of a leader's job no matter where we are. But we must acknowledge some nuances and adjust if we are to be effective Long-Distance Leaders.

Here are some factors we leaders need to be aware of, and adjust to, in the new world of work.

Employee Engagement

Organizations have long worried about employee engagement. People who are socially, mentally, and physically excited and satisfied do better work and stay on the team longer. They also encourage others, do higher-quality work, and put in more discretionary effort. One concern many senior leaders have about remote work is that people will become disengaged if they aren't surrounded by coworkers and physically interacting with each other. Remember that your culture already includes those who are remote, whether you are conscious of that or not.

During the pandemic, one of the biggest concerns was that people would become disengaged and careless about the quality of their work and relationships with their colleagues. In fact, the opposite happened.

One of our largest clients continued their "voice of the employee" surveys during the chaos of sending everyone home. What they found defied expectations. During the first six months of the Covid period, employee engagement scores shot up and stayed up for most of the year, only returning to pre-pandemic levels as people got used to the new way of working.

Why was that?

There are engagement factors that are more important than whether the mission statement is on the wall where you work or whether everyone is wearing company swag. There was a crisis, and people pitched in. They knew the company needed their best efforts and didn't want to let their teammates or their manager down. They cared about the customers. And, it should be admitted, they wanted to keep their jobs during a period of great turmoil. The more uncertain the world and the work situation was, the more people cared and pulled together. They chose to be engaged, often more than they were during the old status quo.

Since then, we've learned something about remote employees and engagement. Those engaged employees who work remotely some or all the time are the most connected, satisfied employees in the organization. That's the good news. The bad news is that those who are disengaged are more disengaged than those who go to the office every day.

Remember that Outcomes, Others, and Ourselves define our work. Two of those three have changed far more than the third.

Engagement is not something leaders can directly control. It is intrinsic to each individual. We choose to be engaged or not. Long-Distance Leaders must reexamine the actions that encourage people to choose engagement versus distance.

Here are some things in a leader's control:

- Interacting with team members regularly—and in a high-quality, genuine way.

- Creating fair opportunities for career improvement and development with those who work in the office full-time.

- Providing an appropriate mix of positive and corrective feedback. If your team believes people who work with the manager every day get better and more frequent feedback than they get, it can lead to resentment and feelings of isolation.

- Helping all team members feel connected to the team and organization's purpose, values, and rewards (and each other).

Retention and Turnover

It wasn't surprising that the return to the office after the pandemic was chaotic. People who didn't think they could work from home enjoyed the benefits. Some people (especially senior leaders) couldn't wait to get back to the way things were and were surprised by the amount of reluctance they encountered in bringing people back together. Returning to the workplace meant changes in lifestyle, childcare, and even commuting costs. All these things—and more—encouraged people to reexamine their employment situation.

A wave of people started choosing other options. That wave seems to have reached stasis for now, although leaders will always have to consider location and flexibility in the future. The long-distance genie is out of the bottle.

While your engaged teammates aren't likely going anywhere, remote workers who are unhappy are more prone to leaving for other remote jobs. There are simply fewer barriers to leaving when the commute, family care, and office facilities aren't factors in a decision to stay or leave.

It is important that Long-Distance Leaders do the following:

- *Hire people to do the work that needs to be done.* Remote work gives you a chance to expand your hiring pool. Finding the right people for the work makes leading them easier once they're hired.

- *Provide clear expectations of time, place, and the work involved.* Many people hired to work remotely during the pandemic suddenly were told they needed to be in the office. That defied the expectations they had when they were hired and tensions arose.

- *Offer career development* so that all team members, regardless of location, see a future with the team and the organization and choose to stay instead of jumping at the first tempting offer from recruiters.

Building Relationships That Defy Distance

Employees stay and do good work at places they feel appreciated and where they know and like their teammates. As leaders, we must avoid behaviors that can create cracks in the team and consistently act in ways that bring people together. Here are some specific suggestions:

- *Intentionally create connections between those in the office and those who aren't.* It is tempting to let people self-select who they go to for answers or choose to work with to solve problems. Beware of the cliques that can form among those who are together more—and how people can feel (unintentionally) excluded. As leaders, we need to be observant and aware of the team dynamics that are helping—or hurting—working relationships.

- *Take distance into account on all teambuilding activities.* Ordering pizza for the big meeting might make sense, but what message does that send to the people who are attending virtually? Do your team activities consider everyone and give the remote people an equal chance of participating and feeling connected?

- *Use technology effectively.* We'll discuss this explicitly in future chapters, but it's important that the tools you use allow people to take part fully in the team's work and support social connections and task completion. A good example is creating a "water cooler" group on Teams or Slack where people can tell jokes, tease each other about sports teams, or share family news. Encourage people in the office to use their webcam when talking to remote peers because it might not cross their minds.

Tending to Ourselves

Like Alisha in our example, you may find that leading at a distance takes a toll on you. Even if we're completely confident in our abilities (and how many of us are?) it's hard to ensure we're at our best for our team.

As hybrid work takes off, leaders often find themselves stretched thin. Flexible time is great for employees, but it may mean your day begins earlier and ends later than everyone else's. You have work that needs to be done, but being in the office and having people constantly buzzing around doesn't allow you to focus and get your own tasks completed.

Too many leaders sacrifice their own time and energy for the sake of their team. Whether you consider it the price of servant leadership, or just taking one for the team, you may find yourself exhausted, distracted, and inefficient.

Here are some ideas for taking care of yourself and your mental/physical health:

- *Protect your time.* What expectations do you have for your employees to respond to messages after hours? Do you expect them to ignore their families or work hours they aren't compensated for? Surely you want them to take their assigned vacation and personal time. Do the same for yourself. Be clear with your team when you are on (and off) the clock.

- *Model realistic expectations and behavior.* Use and stand by your out-of-office notifications and status updates. If you choose to write emails during off hours, set your system to send them out at a specific time in the morning so your team isn't getting messages in the middle of the night and reacting in a panic.

- *Make time for your team.* Remote employees can't poke their heads into your office to see if you're available or catch you on the way to the coffee machine. Try setting up office hours where, for a few hours a week, you are available to those who aren't in the office. This will give them a sense that you care about them as much as those you share space with. It will reduce the number of out-of-the-blue interruptions because they know when you are available to them.

■ *Schedule rest and exercise, and eat like a grownup.* As the old saying goes, you aren't any good to anyone if you're not good to yourself. This sounds obvious, but leaders are used to thinking of themselves and their own needs last. Nobody will begrudge your taking care of yourself, and it may even inspire others to do the same.

■ *Continue to learn and grow.* Your employees are engaged and energized when they have fresh challenges and chances to learn new skills. Why are you any different? Training can make you better, faster, and more efficient. It is also fun and gives your brain a chance to think about something new. Too many leaders don't take advantage of learning opportunities because they're too busy or don't want to spend the budgets. Don't think of it as a cost. Consider it an investment in yourself and your team.

Pause and Reflect

Ask yourself these questions:

▶ How has long-distance work affected me personally?

▶ Am I more stressed? Less stressed? What in particular impacts me?

▶ What is one thing I can do to be more effective in leading others?

▶ What is one area in which I need to be better to myself?

Chapter 10

Hybrid Work and Long-Distance Leaders

Rule 10: If you have one remote team member, you have a Long-Distance Team.

Success in a hybrid work environment requires employers to move
beyond viewing remote or hybrid environments as a temporary
or short-term strategy and to treat it as an opportunity.

—George Penn, Managing Vice President, Gartner

Joon has been put in charge of a hybrid IT team that was put together post-pandemic. Everyone lives in the area but can choose whether to come into the office full time or not. Most work remotely one or two days a week. The team's productivity is fine, but Joon's concerned about team cohesion and morale. To allow people flexibility, she allows them to pick their schedule as much as the company will allow. Despite her flexibility, she's heard complaints that she's favoring the people who come into the office most. She's becoming frustrated and is tempted to just tell everyone to come in full time.

The Rise of Hybrid Work and What It Means for Leaders

Before the Covid pandemic, remote work was on the rise. *Telework*, as some called it then, was increasing 25 percent per year.[1] Some organizations were inching into remote work by allowing people to work from home occasionally, but it was largely ad hoc, and done on a team-by-team basis with little formal structure or oversight.

We should be focused on *what* people do, *how* they do it, and *when* the work takes place.

Then Covid came, and overnight thousands of people who had never worked remotely, or even thought about it, were working from home.

As people returned to the office post-pandemic, we saw organizations attempt to put formal structure around who works where, and when. Most companies call it *hybrid work*. In most cases, the term is a catch-all for teams that allow some in-office work and some remote, in several different combinations:

- The team agrees (or policy dictates) to work in the office a set number of days a week and can work remotely the rest of the time. Sometimes these days are assigned; other times people choose when they work from home.

- The team is free to choose where they work, but there are strict rules about when work begins and ends. Work is essentially synchronous, with everyone in the office or online for the same hours a day.

- Some of the team is in the office, some of the team works remotely, there are few restrictions on the time or place, and most of the work is asynchronous.

As you can imagine, these work arrangements create several challenges for leaders. If remote leadership is mostly like leading traditionally, with some nuances and differences, hybrid work is leading with a very specific twist. It is leading in person *and* remote *at the same time*. It can feel like you have the benefits—and the challenges—of both workplaces.

This feeling of being betwixt and between is complicated by the fact these arrangements are often informal. They're negotiated at the team level between the manager and the teammate. In other cases, the agreement isn't informal but is imposed organizationally—whether individual leaders agree or not. In these situations, leaders don't feel like they are fully supported by the organization and feel that there's a lack of guidance. But this doesn't have to be the case.

We would be remiss in this new edition if we didn't address an important fact about hybrid work. What many people call *hybrid* isn't an intentional organizational choice but more of an uncomfortable compromise. It's a negotiated agreement in which the company gets people back in the office with enough flexibility that people aren't entirely unhappy or threatening to quit.

A lot of employers just wanted to get back to "normal," after the events of the early 2020s. But after working remotely for so long, many people were not comfortable simply returning to the office as though nothing had changed. There was a period of upheaval where we had what was called the Great Resignation. People simply chose to quit and find jobs where they could work remotely. Those who did return were often unhappy about it.

Hybrid work is most successful when it is an intentional, conscious way of organizing the team's work.

True and Effective Hybrid Work

The word *hybrid* is often taken to mean a blend of things. In biology a hybrid is a mix of two parents that results in an entirely new thing. A horse and a donkey create a mule. Anyone who's ever worked with mules knows they have traits of both parents but are a unique animal.

The same is true of hybrid work. Ideally, a good hybrid working arrangement is not exactly like being in the office, nor is it the same as when people are fully remote. It should be a method of working that combines the best traits of both in new and exciting ways. It should offer people the opportunity for in-person or synchronous communication that can make in-person work so valuable while taking advantage of the opportunities offered by remote work.

When organizations take a blended approach, it usually winds up looking like a simulation of the in-office experience. Team members are told, "you can work from home, but we expect you to keep office hours and be available at the same time as your teammates." When it works, synchronous technology keeps everyone connected. Webcams, chat, and old-fashioned phone calls allow for brainstorming, communicating, and building relationships that mimic the way we worked when everyone was together.

The downside? We spend a lot of time in meetings, whether in person or virtual, because we think we must work synchronously. It can be difficult to do focused work when we're constantly interrupted (and interrupting each other) with emails, instant messages, and Zoom calls. Any advantages of remote work, such as the ability to focus away from the noisy office, are counterbalanced by always having to be available and on call.

True hybrid work is not simply determined by where people work; it includes the dimension of time too. It focuses on *what* people do, *how* they do it, and *when* the work takes place. Such work is less time-bound and more focused on getting the best results, no matter where people are working, and on making sure the team functions at a high level that makes the most of both the office environment and a flexible working arrangement.

The Challenges of Hybrid Work for Leaders

In addition to the challenges of long-distance work we've been talking about, leaders face some nuances in hybrid work as well. These differences can be addressed with the same thought and intentionality that fully remote work requires; leaders just need to be aware of them.

Here are the most common challenges:

■ Knowing who is where, when, and up to what

- Keeping the team engaged

- Creating one team and avoiding cliques

- Overcoming proximity bias

- Balancing the work done remotely and in-office

Communication is the key to successful outcomes on any team. Remote work is challenging but can be successful when technology is effectively used. On hybrid teams, especially when people may have irregular schedules, it's important team members know where their teammates are working, when they are available, and how best to work together in those moments.

It can be frustrating to plan a conversation with someone only to find out it's not their day in the office. Good hybrid teams share calendars and schedules so they can maintain workflow, get answers to questions, and help each other be productive. Leaders are responsible for helping to create and enforce these processes so people can do their best work.

Engagement is always an issue on any team, but we've found there's a paradox at play on hybrid teams. Those who work in the office are more engaged than most employees. Those who are primarily or frequently remote and feel connected, energized, and productive are perhaps the most engaged employees you have. The bad news is that those who are remote and don't feel that way, those who feel isolated, are the least engaged employees and most at risk for turnover or poor performance.

A leading reason for disconnection and a lack of enthusiasm occurs when people feel they are not valued or have been left out. That's true in any workplace. But when we don't share a workplace with our teammates, disengagement becomes even more likely. On hybrid teams, there's an added wrinkle—it's not uncommon for cliques to form. People in the office naturally tend to go first to the people they are physically close to for advice, social interaction, and help with the work. It's not that they don't like or appreciate their remote teammates, it's just easier to turn to the person at the next desk.

Over time, cliques form. The people who are in the office less frequently might feel excluded from the "in-crowd," or they may think that the in-office teammates are getting advantages they don't receive. The people in the office, on the other hand, sometimes resent the remote workers. They don't have to commute, or wear business clothes, and they can avoid the boss's unwanted attention. It can be difficult to create a one-team environment when people have different workplace circumstances.

For leaders, perhaps the biggest challenge is proximity bias. It is both practical and natural to turn to the person in front of you when you have a question. If something needs to be done, you delegate it to the person who's in the office with you. Sometimes it's for convenience; sometimes it's because you see that person at work and know they can do the job (or it will be easier for you to coach them).

The problem with this (mostly) unconscious prejudice is that some members of the team may feel excluded while others feel under a microscope. They might think you are exhibiting favoritism to the people you see all the time. Remote workers already feel they get less-effective feedback when they don't share a location with their boss. Now imagine what happens if they think others are getting more of your time and coaching just because they are in the office with you.

The perception of favoritism or discrimination is as toxic as the real thing. Long-Distance Leaders need to be aware of how they interact and create equitable access for all team members.

Finally, challenges in hybrid workplaces are potential barriers to productivity and team morale. One of the biggest complaints about the return to office has been, "I can't get anything done because there's too much socializing and noise and I'm constantly interrupted." One of the hallmarks of successful hybrid teams is rethinking what work gets done when and in what locations.

Many teams encourage meetings and face-to-face interaction for days when people are in the office together and discourage meetings when people are working elsewhere. No Meeting Fridays are becoming a thing—and a good one unless that is the day everyone is in the office. True, people may not get as many individual tasks completed when they're in the office, but they can, if planned, accomplish group work during that time. Coaching sessions should be planned for when you have a better chance of meeting face to face and having more focused, impactful conversations.

The Advantages of Hybrid Work

If it sounds like it's too much work to put together a hybrid strategy, or that it is complex and not worth it, we beg to differ. Although we've never advocated solely for "remote" work nor "in-office only," similarly we don't think hybrid is the only or best solution. It can, however, be a great option when implemented correctly.

Here are some major advantages to working in this new way:

- You can reap the benefits of both remote work and in-office.

- You can expand your hiring pool.

- You can create more flexibility and work/life balance, which have long-reaching effects on engagement and retention.

- You can improve meetings, collaboration, and outcomes with more effective asynchronous work.

As a leader, you know there are different workstyles, and every member of your team has their own way of doing things. Good leaders see that as a strength rather than as a problem. If you have a team where people are expected to be in the office a certain number of days a week, help them optimize their time. Meetings, teambuilding activities, and important conversations should be as effective and "rich" as possible (more on richness in an upcoming chapter).

Task completion can be difficult in a noisy office, so in-office days aren't the best time for people to focus on checking things off their list that require uninterrupted "think time." Introverts get the quiet time they need when away from the office while extroverts still get social contact and birthday cake in the breakroom. Collaborate with your team to agree on what work gets done where to get the best possible outcomes.

Organizations that restrict remote work are often at a disadvantage when recruiting and keeping staff. Long commutes (or the need to come to the office at all) can limit your employment pool to people who live within a specific geographic area. Remote work vastly expands that area, and even a couple of days in the office may appeal to people willing to fight traffic a day or two a week, while working from home the rest.

We don't want you to look at hybrid work as merely a compromise where you let people work from home just enough so they don't quit, but that can be *part* of the strategy. For years people who work hard, physical labor have experimented with different shifts and availability. You probably know a police person or firefighter who works five on, four off, or some similar arrangement. There's no reason similar flexibility can't work in knowledge work.

Remember, one of the huge differentiators between remote, in-office, and hybrid work is time flexibility. Flexibility, once seen as a perk, has become more expected in the post-pandemic view of work. As important, this flexibility can create greater productivity and mental health.

As an example, let's take meetings, and how they've been run for most of your career. People show up (online or in person) and the meeting begins. Maybe people are prepared for what's going to be discussed, maybe not. It takes a while to get to the point, people begin to talk, sometimes to argue. Then a decision is reached, and you move on. Sounds normal and often efficient. But are these meetings really efficient?

Let's rethink such a meeting. What if everyone had a real opportunity, before the meeting, to think about the topic and prepare their thoughts and ideas? This would give everyone the chance to share their thinking in the way that serves them best. A virtual meeting can allow verbal and written input in the form of chat or submitted documents. Then, after the meeting, the team can use a Slack or Teams channel to offer questions or thoughts that occurred to them after the meeting. This increases the quality of the input while limiting the amount of time wasted in the meeting.

This is only one way that asynchronous tools allow people to use time efficiently and do their best thinking when it works for them. If, like Wayne, you are on a later time zone than the rest of the team, you are sometimes in meetings that are called before your brain is awake. Similarly, late afternoon meetings might be hard on your body clock. What if you got your assignment and did the work when your thinking was clear or when you had the time to really invest in thinking about the situation?

What separates true hybrid from other options is recognizing time as a factor in ways that it has never been possible before. The important thing to understand is that the workplace is always changing. Your team structure and policy may need to be reassessed, reexamined, and adjusted as time and circumstances demand. Such changes should also be done in consultation with all the stakeholders; do not just impose them because it seems like a good idea now.

This chapter was added to the book post-Covid because we had to acknowledge how work has evolved in the first part of the twenty-first century. Many teams are rethinking what it means to go to work. If you want a deeper look at how to rethink your team's work and culture, we invite you to check out *The Long-Distance Team: Designing Your Team for Everyone's Success*.

Pause and Reflect

Ask yourself these questions:

▶ As a leader, how well is your in-office/remote work strategy working? What's going well and what needs to be reexamined?

▶ If you have a hybrid team with people in the office a set number of days a week, have you been intentional about what work gets done where, maximizing the in-person time and allowing remote work to be done in ways that get better outcomes?

▶ How can you use asynchronous work to plan, conduct, and follow up on meetings so that you get the best thinking and results from every team member?

Chapter 11

Understanding and Building Trust at a Distance

Rule 11: Building trust at a distance doesn't happen by accident.

Few things can help an individual more than to place responsibility on him, and to let him know that you trust him.

—Booker T. Washington, educator and author

Liz has always prided herself on being a leader who could build trust—it was part of what made her a successful leader. But once she began leading a dispersed team, she felt lost. She wanted to build the sort of positive relationships she always had, but now she had new team members she didn't know, and seldom saw. She struggled until she began to understand the dynamics of trust differently. Once she had a bigger picture, she was more successful with her new remote team, although she still struggles to treat remote workers equally.

Trust is invaluable to leaders. We need to be able to trust the people we lead, and they certainly need to trust us. Jim Kouzes and Barry Posner, authors of *The Leadership Challenge*, have written widely on the importance of trust, as have countless others.[1] Your experience tells you that when people trust you, and you trust them, things work better, more work gets done, and it gets done faster.

When your team is working remotely, it's foolish to say that trust is *more* important than it is when you are all working in the same location. What's different when working remotely is that trust is harder to build and more easily broken. And in hybrid teams there is the added challenge of proximity bias. Even worse, the results of that lack of trust may not be immediately visible, and the damage may be irreparable.

The Trust Triangle

Whether we're talking about a romantic couple, your circle of friends, or that project team you inherited, trust is built—and destroyed—in the same ways. There have been many studies of the subject, and plenty of models have been created. At The Kevin Eikenberry Group, we looked at the metadata and decided that the research could be boiled down to three components necessary for high levels of trust to exist: common purpose, competence, and motives (Figure 9). The more alignment these three components are, the more trust will exist.

Figure 9: The Trust Triangle

The Trust Components in Action

Say you have a friend you play cards with regularly. You are connected by that common purpose so you have trust in that area (you both love playing the game and enjoy each other's company). If you both have *competence* in the game (you both know the rules, have a similar level of skill and strategy, and can play the game fairly) and see that in each other, trust will build further. And as long as you both feel your *motives* are congruent (you want to play the game fairly and see who wins), trust will be high in this area too. But if you find out that your friend is cheating—that their motives for playing the game aren't the same as yours—trust will be reduced. At best you won't want to play cards with that person anymore, and at worst you may never speak to them again. The components of the Trust Triangle explain it all.

Here are some leadership examples, in the form of questions.

- *Common purpose.* Do you and the people you lead have the same purpose? Are you "pulling on the same end of the rope?" If people get the sense that you are not sincere in your beliefs, or they begin to question the organization's goals and behaviors, this may suffer.

- *Competence.* Do you believe that the people you lead are competent? Are they capable of doing what you ask of them? Do your employees believe that you can deliver on your promises? If sales targets are ridiculously high and people come to believe that you don't know what you're talking about or are incapable of doing what you say you will do, there will be a lack of trust. Does your project team understand all you are doing to coordinate and create results even when the project frustration level is high?

- *Motives.* Finally, you might all have the same goals, and everyone is technically capable of acting appropriately, but are they willing to go the extra mile? Do you have your employee's back, or will you always side with the company? Do you do what you say you'll do, or do people suspect you're just telling them what they want to hear?

All these questions and situations apply regardless of where we work. Like most everything else, the factors for building trust are the same as when we're together, but people think about them differently and it becomes harder to trust when we aren't near each other.

How Working Remotely Impacts Trust

In a perfect world, there would be no difference between whether you work with someone down the hall, work far away from them, or only see them occasionally. You both have jobs to do. You do yours, they do theirs, and neither party loses any sleep about what's happening. Yet in our work with clients, we hear all kinds of concerns from team members that are rooted in a lack of trust:

- "How will I know they're working if I can't see them?"

- "The people in the home office get all the attention and promotions."

- "The people working from home have it great; they don't have to do all the dirty little jobs and the manager leaves them alone to get their work done. We are in eyesight, so she comes to us first and leaves the teleworkers alone."

One of the most dramatic stories we've encountered took place when Wayne was discussing the use of webcams as a means of building trust. One of the participants in a session informed him that they didn't use webcams, and in fact it was common practice to put tape or sticky notes over the cameras, even when they weren't in use. When Wayne asked why, the participant answered, "because they only want us to use webcams so they can make sure we're working, and we don't want them (management) spying on us." How bad is the level of trust in an organization if people are refusing to use communication tools because they believe the organization is watching them all the time? On the other hand, if your organization is doing this, trust is already a legitimate issue, and we'd encourage you to work on that as soon as possible.

An Example

Helen has two coworkers. She's worked with Gretchen in the past and knows that even though Gretchen doesn't say much in meetings, she's diligent, and when she does speak, it's always useful. Also, in all the time Helen has known her, she's never seriously missed a deadline or failed to honor a commitment. Helen trusts Gretchen implicitly.

Meanwhile, Rajesh is new to the team and he and Helen have never met in person. She knows nothing about him, except that he's occasionally spoken on conference calls and seems smart enough. But she notices he missed his last deadline.

When working remotely, it's foolish to say that trust is *more* important than it is when you are all working in the same location. What's different when working remotely is that trust is harder to build and more easily broken.

Who does Helen trust less? The problem (probably) doesn't lie solely with Rajesh. Anyone could miss a deadline, but Helen is making her judgment about his competence, alignment to the group, and motivation based on a very small amount of data. If she's a naturally trusting person, she might cut him some slack. But if she's paranoid, or in a hurry, or just in a bad mood, she's going to go with the person she *knows* she can trust. She might even decide she's never going to Rajesh for help with anything—which won't help build trust with him or change her initial perception.

One bad experience probably won't have the same impact on her relationship with Gretchen because there's a built-up stockpile of experience and trust.

In Real Life

This happens in remote teams all the time. When you send out an instant message (IM) cry for help, Joanne always answers in a hurry, so you note that she's obviously motivated to help. When you send a similar IM to Bob, he takes all day to respond, so you assume he doesn't care if you live or die. That's likely unfair. Maybe Bob has been in a meeting all day, or he wanted to make sure he came up with the absolute best answer before responding. All you know is that with the data available, you've decided to trust Joanne more than Bob, and over time she becomes your go-to for answers. This becomes even more prevalent if you work onsite the same days as Joanne does.

Trust is evidence-based. Without evidence, we must guess whether we can trust people. If you assume positive intent, that will help, but what do you do when something happens to shake your trust? For most people it's easier to damage trust than rebuild it.

When working remotely, even some of the time, you have fewer opportunities to assess whether someone's really aligned with your purpose, is competent at their job, and is as motivated as you are. When you work in the same location, you see them come in early and leave late, you see them taking notes in meetings. You know that if you have a question about X, Inez is the person to talk to. But when you don't really know the people you work with, it's difficult to build a strong, trusting work relationship.

Intentionally Building Trust at a Distance

Trust can be built at a distance or with infrequent face-to-face interaction, but it doesn't happen by accident. Give people opportunities to see that everyone is aligned on the three corners of the Trust Triangle: common purpose, competence, and motives. Creating and helping build this alignment with the three corners of the Trust Triangle is an important part of your job. Once people know who they're working with, how smart their fellow team members are, and that they are all headed to the same destination, they will work in a trusting manner.

When working remotely, the team doesn't interact as much as they would in person. Frequently, communication goes through you as the leader and the team doesn't have nearly as many chances to see each other in action. That's why a Long-Distance Leader does some very practical things to help build trust as a team and between team members. Consider this list:

- *Use meetings strategically.* One of the unfortunate side effects of our 24/7 world is that time has become too precious to waste. The nature of web meetings makes this even more true. Meetings may be the only time teammates speak to each other as a group. This is why many teams schedule more meetings now than ever before. According to Microsoft, there are up to eighty million Teams meetings a day, about the same as during the pandemic, but the number of in-person meetings has gone up as well, so we're meeting more than ever.[2] Build in time for people to really see how smart the team is. You could try showcasing one person per meeting, letting them talk about their work, or highlighting their strengths for them ("If you guys have a question about Excel, Inez can help"). Or do quick introductions each week, allowing people to get answers to questions or challenges they face. Nothing shows motivation like someone helping solve a problem. Use all the keys to great meetings, including agendas, but remember that with a remote team these meetings do more than communicate and get the work done—they are a time that trust can be built.

- *Share praise in public.* As a leader, you know that positive feedback is important (and we talked much more about this and feedback in general in Chapter 8). Unfortunately, in a virtual world that might happen one on one. That feedback makes the person feel good, but the rest of the team doesn't hear what a fine job they did on the Jackson account, or how hard they worked to help everyone meet that deadline. We need to help the team learn each other's strengths, talents, and efforts.

- *Delegate in public.* When assigning tasks, the perception of fairness is as important as equality itself. Often remote teams don't know what others are working on. This can lead to a sense that "those folks" are being spared the dirty jobs you're making others do. When you delegate or assign projects, let the whole team know who's doing what. While you likely won't do the delegation on your call/meeting ("Adrienne, I want you to . . ."), it might help if you let everyone on the team know that you have handed that specific task to Adrienne.

■ *Intentionally create opportunities the team members can use to get to know and build trust with each other.* Leaders can help their people get to know each other by intentionally mixing up teams, assigning mentors, and delegating some of the training between team members. This creates chances for teammates to interact with those they might not otherwise work with closely. On hybrid teams, make decisions about what work happens where. Think about using time together for meetings or work that requires collaboration in order to strengthen team bonds. Heads-down, isolated work can take place when people aren't together. Don't sacrifice opportunities to build team trust in the interest of "getting back to work."

■ *Use technology to build relationships.* We all work best with people we know, like, and trust. But how do we get to know each other? Synchronous tools allow people to work together regardless of connection. We will say it again, encourage the use of webcams, especially one on one, even when some people are in the office. You can also use asynchronous tools like Slack or Teams to showcase task status and expertise. If your team is large or spread across many time zones, consider Q&A forums where people who don't speak to each other can still offer help and insight to their teammates.

■ *If you see something, say something.* There are plenty of signs that trust may be an issue on the team. If you're suddenly deluged with email and are being copied on every communication, that could be a sign of trouble. This might be a person's way of letting you know what they are working on, or perhaps that they don't trust the other person, and they think including you in the email thread will ensure a response. Watch especially for signs of proximity bias where people are unintentionally favoring those who spend more time in the office. When you see behavior that might indicate a problem, be proactive to identify what's really happening, help people clarify the situation, and help them build connections, reduce conflict, and if necessary, reset expectations.

Remember that trust is easily broken and hard to mend. It also can't be done unilaterally. Frequent, candid conversations with both your team as a whole and individual members can help avoid problems. As Napoleon once said, "if you want to avoid war, avoid the thousand little pinpricks that lead to war."

Pause and Reflect

Ask yourself these questions:

▶ Do I see signs of eroding trust on my team? What are they?

▶ When I look at the Trust Triangle, which factor(s) seem to be out of whack on my team?

▶ How can I strengthen areas of weakness?

Online Resource

To better understand your starting point on trust and how to build it more effectively with others, register at LongDistanceWorklife.com/Resources and request The Trust Thermostat Tool or use this QR code.

Chapter 12

Choosing the Right Communication Tools

Rule 12: Identify the leadership results you need, then select the communication tool to achieve them.

The medium is the message because it is the medium that shapes and controls the scale and form of human association and action.

—Marshall McLuhan, professor and media critic

Theresa laments that it used to be easy when everyone worked in the office together. You had face-to-face communication, meetings, and a controllable amount of email and chat. Now, with people working everywhere, the tools she needs to master require two hands to count. Some of the tools she isn't sure how to use, some she has never seen used well, and some, well, she just doesn't like. Since it's tough to schedule face to face, she leans on email and Teams meetings far too often, even though she knows it causes a time crunch.

We've been saying throughout the book that Long-Distance Leadership is *mostly* the same as traditional leadership except for the pesky technology. That's an awfully small hinge swinging a terribly big door.

You may have a complicated relationship with technology. If you've been around long enough, you have gone through two or three generations of tools already. You realize that while new technology may solve one problem, nothing fixes every issue (and sometimes it creates a whole new set of unexpected headaches). And even if you are competent with the current tools, you know they will continue to change.

These things are most assuredly true:

- Things change quickly when it comes to communication technology.

- Unless you own the company, the decision over what's available to you is probably not yours alone.

- No one has explicitly set expectations on the best ways to communicate with your team (and if you don't know, your team members don't either).

- Picking the right tools affects more than just simply delivering information. You must consider how you want to get your message across and how you can receive feedback on that message effectively. From a see-and-be-seen perspective, choosing the right tool for the job is critical.

The timing of the Covid pandemic was a perfect storm of all these reasons. New tools like Zoom became available, and people grabbed at them. It soon became obvious that the problem wasn't a lack of tools. In fact, there were too many. Toward the end of 2021, Teams offered a single solution to some of this, imperfect as it may be. The whiplash of changing, canceling, and learning tools caused no end to the headaches.

The available tools, and the way they're used, also affect how we create and nurture trust. If your team is scattered across time zones but the only way they talk to each other is synchronous, how are the people in India expected to demonstrate their competence and motivation to the people in Los Angeles, who are asleep when they're doing their best work?

We want to help you improve your judgment and make better tool-selection decisions. It starts with a simple tool that we use in many of our programs to help people focus their thinking about which tool to use when (and how).

For communication to be effective and appropriate, you want to strike the right balance between richness and scope.

In 2001, the Swiss/German researcher Bettina Büchel created a simple matrix that we think explains this concept as well as anything we've seen (see Figure 10).[1] In order for communication to be effective and appropriate, you want to strike the right balance between richness and scope.

Here's what that model looks like:

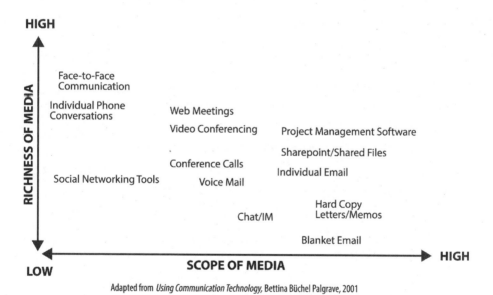

Adapted from *Using Communication Technology,* Bettina Büchel Palgrave, 2001

Figure 10: Richness and Scope in Communication

Let's look at what this model means in your daily work as a Long-Distance Leader.

Richness

True communication is more than simply understanding the content of a message, regardless of how it's transmitted. We all know humans communicate in multiple ways. Our tone of voice, the expression on our faces, our body language, and the words we choose all help us to project a seemingly simple message.

When someone says, "I'm fine," are they really? Maybe they can't look you in the eye as they say it, or the way they say it indicates that they don't really believe everything is good. If you're next to them, and you can gather all those clues, you can better assess if they really are fine or if you need to probe further to make sure there isn't something more you need to know.

With Büchel's model, the best example of rich communication is one on one, in person. You and the other person are in physical proximity, you can see and hear each other, and you're getting all the nonverbal, visual, and social cues you need to interpret the other person's message. And you can ensure that yours is understood and accepted as well.

The problem is that these perfect circumstances rarely happen during your time as a Long-Distance Leader. Beyond the obvious distance challenges, both time and the sheer number of people involved impact this too. If your group is large, for example, even if you're face to face, people may not speak up or ask questions. As the group size grows, it is very common for the communication to become a broadcast, with people holding questions until the end rather than letting those questions emerge organically—if they ask them at all. If you've ever been on a teleconference or web meeting and asked, "Any questions?" only to be met with the sound of crickets, you've experienced this phenomenon.

Hybrid work creates different challenges. There will be times when most or all of the team members are in the office together and times they're scattered to the wind. One of the important skills for leaders in this new workplace is to use the time together for communication that is best done live and in person. This may mean changing what work gets done where. Ignoring this may lead to even more meetings than ever—and nobody wants that. We need better communication, not more of it.

Richness suffers over time and space. Twenty-four hours after a meeting, if you ask two people who've been part of the same conversation what they took away from it, you're likely to get very different interpretations. It's impractical to get face to face every time we need to communicate with somebody. In fact, with people scattered all over the place, it defies the laws of physics, not to mention economics! So every time we pick up the phone or fire off an email rather than getting into the car, or hold a videoconference instead of hopping on a plane, we're sacrificing richness in favor of scope.

Scope

That need to account for time and distance is where scope comes in. Email is the perfect example of a tool with great scope. Thousands of people receive the same message at the same time (theoretically, at least). You can't see the reactions of your readers, hear their wails of anguish or shouts of joy, or answer their questions in real time. You don't know if you've been understood correctly or if people have bought in. And let's be honest, you don't even know if they've read the darn thing.

That's not to say that richness is superior to scope. The ability to reference past communication and make information consistent across readers and locations is important. We also know that if you've spent three days apologizing for a message that took thirty seconds to write, you understand that scope carries its own set of limitations and constraints.

Finding the Right Mix

If you look at the matrix in Figure 10, you'll see that nearly every method of communication strikes some balance between richness and scope. To have rich conversations, you may need to sacrifice time and efficiency. You can save time by dashing off an email, but you do so at the risk of being misinterpreted, or of having people needing answers to questions they have before they can implement your suggestion.

Too often Long-Distance Leaders are so busy doing the job, they aren't as mindful as they need to be about which tools they use and how effective they are. Remember the Remote Leadership Model in Chapter 4? As a leader, be mindful of your messages and communication goals, then choose the right tool for the task.

Web meetings are a good example. Let's say you have Teams as your daily collaboration tool. As Figure 10 shows, web meetings are in the middle ground—fairly rich, with good scope. In fact, depending on how they are used, they can be quite high in richness (e.g., one-on-one video calls, coaching, and training) or have terrific scope (the dreaded but often useful "all hands meeting"). But generally, you sacrifice one factor for the other based on how you use the tool.

If you need to brainstorm effectively, you might want to have small groups using webcams and/or breakout rooms and full participation with the online whiteboard. You may even want to record the meeting for later use or to include those who couldn't attend. These uses lead to surprisingly rich communication.

On the other hand, if you're not using webcams and have a hundred people online, you might get your message out (high scope!) but will have little real chance of engaging people, getting input, answering questions in real time, or gauging your participants' reactions. That's where Slack and unique chat rooms for specific teams and topics can help you brainstorm asynchronously.

This doesn't make that big web meeting wrong; it might be the best way to communicate the message at hand. The point is to be mindful of what you're trying to get across, to whom, and how "richly" it needs to be done.

Often leaders choose one tool over the other for both good and bad reasons. Situationally, relying on email and text messages may make sense when you are traveling and crossing time zones, but if the message is sensitive, complex, or easily misinterpreted, are you sacrificing effectiveness for convenience? Similarly, if you're coaching an employee on the phone, is it because that's the only way to have that conversation, or because one or both of you are uncomfortable with webcams and would rather not use them? (Even though it would be incredibly helpful for you to see each other's facial expressions and body language.)

Long-Distance Leaders can't avoid this important new part of the job. You must be aware of the tools at your disposal and understand their advantages and disadvantages; then you can use them to their maximum potential.

Pause and Reflect

Look at Figure 10. Ask yourself the following questions:

▶ Which tools are my team and I using well?

▶ Which tools do I default to?

▶ Which tools are my team and I not using well?

▶ Are there tools we don't have that would be helpful?

▶ Are there tools we have that we're not utilizing due to a lack of training or knowledge?

▶ If we used those tools, how might the way I communicate and build trust be impacted (positively and negatively)?

▶ What am I going to do about it?

Chapter 13

Technology Tips for the Long-Distance Leader

Rule 13: Maximize a tool's capabilities or you'll minimize your effectiveness.

Any sufficiently advanced technology should be indistinguishable from magic.
—Arthur C. Clarke, author

James is surprised when he realizes all the communication tools he has at his disposal, and how few of them he uses or is comfortable with. He remembers the days when the big decision was choosing between voicemail and email. Now that his team is hybrid, there's even more confusion. Some team members rely more than ever on face-to-face communication. Meetings are often the in-office team in a conference room and those working remotely connecting electronically, but this feels unsatisfactory. New tools like Teams or Slack have emerged, but people seem to use the least possible number of features. Considering the challenges he and his team face, he is sure some of these constantly changing tools hold answers, but he doesn't know where to start, which ones to use, or where to focus his limited time to learn more.

Many leaders have a difficult relationship with electronic communication tools. As we've pointed out already, this is a bigger challenge for the Long-Distance Leader because so much is mediated by digital communication. The natural place to start is by asking, "*What* needs to be communicated?" If form follows function, *how* you choose to communicate should be clear.

Give yourself permission to acknowledge that some of this may be new and uncomfortable. Leaders, particularly senior leaders, struggle to use technology successfully for three reasons:

- *There's no pain.* They have been very successful without using these tools in the past, so they either discount the tools' importance or put off using them, succumbing to the "tyranny of fine," believing there are bigger problems to solve right now.

- *It doesn't seem "natural."* Most leaders are not digital natives. Leaders are often older and less technically savvy than others on their teams.[1] This can often make them feel incompetent, or at least less confident than they'd like to be, and thus they avoid using many of the available tools.

- *It keeps changing.* It is true that technology changes so fast many of us are too busy trying to get the job done to be aware of all the latest gadgets and innovations. This can create a vicious cycle of getting further and further behind in utilizing the available tools to maximize communication and organizational results.

Remember this: *not* using these tools isn't a viable option. With the return-to-office mandates and more hybrid work, it's tempting to think you can just go back to how things worked when everyone was in the office all the time. But when you realize you must build trust, communicate clearly, and have productive meetings, you will realize you need to use the technology at your disposal. This requires choosing the right tool for the right job (by balancing richness and scope) and then using it as effectively as possible. If you don't, you are trying to do hard work with one hand tied behind your back.

Be honest with yourself—you may not be an expert in the use of one or more of the tools or technologies available to you. Every manager we speak to understands that tools like Zoom, Teams, or Slack are "mission critical" in keeping remote teams connected. Very few feel "confident and competent" using those tools. Technology changes too fast, and training has been spotty or inconsistent at best.

The good news is you don't have to be the biggest power-user on the team. But you *do* need to leverage what's at your disposal well enough to accomplish your goals and maintain your credibility. Think about it this way: you know what you need to communicate, so you must choose the best tools and use them effectively to make the needed communication happen.

> **Choose the right tool for the right job (by balancing richness and scope) and then use it as effectively as possible.**

In this chapter, we're going to look at types of tools and general categories without getting too specific. Partly, this is because we are platform neutral; although we have tools we use internally, we work with most of the available tools to help our clients succeed. Things change fast. After 2020, tools like Zoom rose, became ubiquitous, and have since started to decrease in popularity. Organizations that use Teams have increased 1000 percent since the pandemic. As of 2023, Microsoft reports that the Teams app has been downloaded almost 100 million times.[2] That tool didn't even have the same name when the first edition of this book came out. Remember Skype for Business?

By the time you read this, a specific feature, or brand name, may be completely different. What you need to know is that the vast majority of collaboration platforms have nearly the same features—chat, screen-sharing, webcam integration—even if they are labelled differently. As an important example, whatever platform you are using, you likely have a whiteboard feature. You need to know that is true and that you can use it, and then you need to learn how to use it appropriately.

Before we get to the tools, let's make a clear distinction between two types of communication so that you can use each to your best advantage:

Asynchronous communication allows us to get the information when we need it. In a distributed workplace, a central repository of on-demand information is needed. A virtual file room, with information stored in a variety of ways, is critical. People who miss a meeting or who are sleeping while work goes on in another part of the world can receive the same information the same way, when they need it. This has become even easier with the introduction of artificial intelligence into collaboration tools like Zoom and Teams.

Synchronous communication happens live—at the same time for everyone involved. It's the style you're most familiar—and most comfortable—with since you've been doing it since you drew your first breath. However, in today's dispersed workplace, it is nearly impossible to all be together at the same time (virtually or in the same room). And with hybrid work, you may never know on any given day who will be where and when. As we've mentioned earlier, unlike work where everyone is in the same place at the same time, or each team member is fully remote, hybrid work requires time flexibility. This means we need to be smart about when we rely on synchronous communication. Not everything needs to be shared in a meeting, and not all team members need to be part of every conversation.

Here's why this distinction is important. Think about when leaders call a meeting—everything tends to stop. Work that maybe deserves a higher priority gets put on hold. Now this meeting is an impediment to that work, and an interruption, rather than an asset.

When it comes to getting work done, technology can be both an enabler and a barrier. When the right tool is used in the right way, there is transparency, accountability, and the ability to cross time and space.

The list that follows is by no means exhaustive as new products emerge every day. Stop worrying/complaining about the specific tools your IT department has given you. Chances are, what you have will *get the job done*. And if you use what you have, well, you'll be fine (and be more effective than most). If you are really missing something on this list, share this chapter with (or buy a copy of the book for) your IT leaders.

Asynchronous Tools

Asynchronous tools are those that each team member can access and use on their own. There's no need for everyone to be online or present when everyone else is.

Video and Recorded Messages

Leaders need to see and be seen. Often, we think of asynchronous tools as mostly text-based (message boards, channels, emails), but you can add richness to even casual announcements. Video allows us to add a visual component to our communication. It is almost as easy to push "record" and use video instead of using a broadcast voicemail. It's nice to have high-resolution, well-produced video for big, important announcements, but with the availability of smart phones, as well as Facebook, Snapchat, and other programs, you have no excuse not to show your face on occasion. In fact, casual interaction like this may be more important to building trust than a big production.

. You might store the recordings on your network (more on this in a minute), but there are also plenty of video services you can use that have a secure place to store video, or your IT group can create a place where only your people can access them.

If you don't like seeing yourself on video, or are self-conscious about using webcams, get over yourself. The number one factor in whether a team uses a tool is if their boss uses it. If you're not using your webcam regularly, don't expect your team to either, even if you have told them how important it can be.

Common File Locations

Imagine a file room where every document your team creates is stored, only you don't have to go searching through dusty boxes to find them, and identifying the latest version is as simple as clicking a link. Tools like Microsoft SharePoint, Google Docs, shared drives, and other products like Basecamp allow a permanent, easily accessible, and searchable central warehouse for information.

For the leader, it's easy to achieve transparency when people can access all your communication; they have newsletters, email blasts, and other written and recorded material on demand. Even if most people won't take advantage of these tools, and it may take some work to get them to use them at all, the fact that you've made the information available is a big step in building trust and holding yourself accountable for your commitments.

Email

Yes, email is an asynchronous tool (although too often it isn't used that way). If you send an email, then sit drumming your fingers waiting for a response, *you're using it wrong.* In fact, you're putting people in an uncomfortable position and perhaps killing productivity. Imagine what your team may be thinking when you send that email. Do you want them to drop what they're doing and respond immediately? Is replying to you more important than meeting a deadline or a commitment to another team member? If you need an instant response, consider a more synchronous tool like the phone, instant messaging, or a text message.

Email is best used when:

- *You need greater scope.* You have many people who need the same message at the same time (delivered in the same way).

- *You need a permanent record.* Email is great for creating a permanent record of what has been communicated. Just ask any lawyer. If you don't want a permanent record, don't use email. Remember it is the law—email can be subpoenaed.

- *The message is complete.* Try using the "head, heart, hands" method. Give them the information you want to share (appeals to their logic), clarify what it means to them (showing empathy and understanding), and then be clear about what you want them to *actually do* as a result of the new information (action steps and timeframe). This way, the reader will understand the facts, you'll connect with them better on an empathetic and emotional level (which will increase buy-in or encourage questions and feedback), and you'll answer the important question, "so what do I do now?"

Synchronous Tools

Synchronous tools include the technology that mimics real-time, face-to-face communication. These are great but aren't the only way for teams to communicate in a hybrid world.

Webcam and Video Chat

We're not talking about recorded messages here (although it's highly likely your platform will make it easy to store video conversations). Webcam and video are really underrated for everyday communication. It is the ultimate remote, one-on-one, see-and-be-seen tool. Using webcam on a regular basis serves many uses for both the leader and the members of the team.

Many people think that webcam is used best to "broadcast" messages, and it's certainly useful for that, but it is probably more useful in one-on-one situations. It's more comfortable for people to use their webcam one on one, rather than with the whole team, regardless of the tool being used. And really, if you think about the value of rich communication, isn't it those personal conversations where body language, tone of voice, and eye contact are most critical?

This format gives your team members a chance to communicate effectively with you. Remember, they want to see and hear you as richly as possible, and they need to communicate their ideas, concerns, and information to you in an effective manner too. Hearing someone agree to take action on the phone isn't the same as seeing the look of excitement—or abject horror—on their face when they do it. This also allows them to see you as a real person, not some disembodied name on an email or an unapproachable character from a recorded video. And if they see you in your AC/DC T-shirt from home, or watch you try to work from an airport, that's not such a bad thing. You're human, after all.

For you as the leader, seeing the people you are speaking with is valuable on three levels:

- *Improving communication.* You are communicating to gain and share information, and/or clarify next steps. It's important that you know you've made your point and that the outcome will be what you want and expect. Without the visual cues, you may suggest something that sounds like a command and then not get the feedback you need to question, adjust, or even decide that what you proposed wasn't such a hot idea to start with.

- *Reducing isolation.* Not only do you *feel* isolated as a leader, in a virtual world, you really *are* isolated. The more richly we can connect with other people, the stronger the bonds we make, the less alone we feel. After all, the loneliness you feel may well be felt by the members of your team too.

- *Building trust.* The richer the communication you have, the easier it is to build trust with others. Conversely, in the absence of visual clues, the development of trust can be slowed or more easily broken.

Using a webcam doesn't need to be a big deal. It's often the push of a button on whatever device we happen to be using. It can be as simple as Apple's FaceTime or Meta's Facebook Live, or part of your work tools like Skype. Teams, Slack, Google Workspace, and most other team collaboration tools have integrated video chat. Use the tools you have, but use them in the best possible ways.

One good way to overcome resistance to using webcams is to form a new habit. Whenever possible, schedule meetings with this question: "Do you want to talk by phone or webcam?" Just leave it open ended. Many people will jump at the chance to connect with you. It will also give you the appearance of comfort with the technology (which may or may not be true, but who's to know?), which adds to your credibility and transparency.

Since we're being transparent, here's a story that took place at The Kevin Eikenberry Group a few years ago. Kevin was convinced that using webcams would add value to our conversations, so he insisted everyone have webcams. Not surprisingly, there was some resistance, so rather than insist every conversation be visual, he allowed people to decide when and if they used their cameras. Some did, some didn't. But there were times when he felt video would aid the discussion, so when the conversation was critical or the subject complex or important, he'd ask people to be on camera. So far, so good, right?

The unintended consequence of this, though, was that people began to wonder: If Kevin wanted to talk to you on webcam, were you in trouble or was there bad news? After all, they thought, if we can usually decide, but then Kevin overrides the choice, then a request to be on webcam from him can't be good news. After some trial and error, we shifted to using webcams often for both casual and important communication. Some people use it frequently, some use it as little as they can, but it's now no longer a big deal (at least Kevin hopes not).

Text Messaging (SMS)

Text messaging and instant messaging (IM) are both synchronous, text-based tools, and they often get grouped together, but they are in fact separate tools that can and should be used in different ways.

Texting utilizes the device your people are most likely to have on them at any time day or night: their mobile phones. Therefore, when your message must have great scope (either a large audience or speed is of the essence), texting works well.

Of course, texting generally is used on mobile phones, not on other devices. This means people must have their phones handy to get (and respond to) the message.

Since text messages are often read in a hurry, they are frequently misinterpreted. According to Verizon, 85 percent of people admit to answering texts in the bathroom[3]; our studies suggest the other 15 percent aren't being entirely truthful. This makes sending a text good for quick attention-getting messages but not particularly useful (and perhaps a problem) when the message requires details or nuance.

Remember these things about texting:

- *Texting can work for business.* It's how a good portion of your team functions in everyday life.

- *You have positional power.* This makes every request or demand on their time feel like a command, whether you mean it that way or not. Proper tone and etiquette here are essential.

- *Texting is best used when the message is time-sensitive.* Most people are now trained like Pavlov's dogs to respond immediately to a text. If you respect people's personal time and expect them to check messages only at certain hours, don't send a text. They'll stop what they're doing and check. It had better be worth it to them. If they don't see it as such, beware, you might be seen as a micromanager, or a command-and-control leader.

If someone is working at home, and you send this text: "Do you have a minute?" most people will say "yes," whether it's true or not, because you're the boss. What might be a legitimate request for information from you (you really want to know if they have time for this conversation and you don't want to interfere with higher priorities) doesn't feel optional to them. If what you're asking is "Do you have time to talk?" always let people know that it's an actual request. Instead of "Do you have a minute?" say something more like, "I have a meeting coming up and need some information. Do you have time to talk, or when is a good time for you?" Yes, it takes a little longer, but it provides much clearer communication as an actual question of curiosity rather than an unspoken demand.

Instant Messaging

Instant messaging tends to be part of a larger communication package and is designed to cross platforms. For example, Kevin and Wayne can only text from our mobile phones, but we can use Slack (our IM tool) from all our devices.

Although it's easy to get attention with a text, and possibly a simple answer to a simple question, instant messaging has several advantages:

- *There's a real keyboard.* Your kids may have double-jointed thumbs, but most of us type more clearly and with greater detail on a real keyboard.

- *You are less likely to be multitasking.* While texting can be done on the run, prolonged text conversations require concentration.

- *People turn it off.* When the message isn't time sensitive, IM is better than a text because people can turn it off. Generally, they consider IM to be work-related and have an easier time closing the application when they're not working and getting the messages when they log back on.

- *It's more integrated with work.* Instant messaging platforms allow you easier access to files, email, and other ways to pass information. While you *can* link documents in text, it's certainly easier to send an attachment by IM, or to flip to a document on your computer screen and copy and paste.

Generally speaking, IM is great for synchronous, detailed conversations that reference other information. It can also be very helpful for quick and informal communication—some of what is missed when people work at a distance from each other.

Telephone and Conference Calls

Whereas the phone may be the tool you "grew up with" in the business world, it seems to have gone out of favor with many people. But remember that the phone can be a useful tool in your communication toolkit: phones are portable, talking on them is quick, and you can get very rich verbal and vocal cues. Plus, now, everyone has their phone tethered to themselves 24/7.

There are also disadvantages to using the phone. When you're on a call, sometimes people can't hear you well, are taking the call where they can't speak openly, or are multitasking. During the blaring of airline announcements, while merging on the freeway, or while waiting for the barista to announce their double caramel soy latte with no foam, their concentration can be sorely lacking.

We don't want to kick the phone or conference calls off our list of options, especially if we're looking for speed and want to make sure we get the message to the right people. Practically, though, there may be richer, better ways to conduct that type of business, such as by using the next tool on our list.

Web Meetings

These tools have become very good alternatives to conference calls and one-on-one telephone chats, with one major caveat: they need to be utilized effectively, and to date, that isn't always the case. It's accepted wisdom in the software and applications space that the average user of any of these platforms uses only 20 percent of their features. Worse, the number of web meetings has tripled since the start of the pandemic. We must be smarter about not just how we meet, but whether there are alternatives to having everyone gather every time something needs to be discussed.

As of this writing, there are fewer collaboration tools than there were previously, but they are used more often. We aren't experts on all of them and you don't have to be either. You need to know this—most of them have the critical features in common; you need to know that the following features exist and how they add value to your meetings:

- Webcams

- Whiteboards to capture vital information and enhance brainstorming and collaboration

- Chat to generate input and ensure people get heard

- Polling or surveying

- File transfer and saving for sharing information in real time

- Breakout rooms for smaller group discussion

If you don't know about these tools, talk to someone in your organization or on your team who uses them well. If you're going to use them in your everyday work, it will be worth getting that person to serve as a mentor.

While it is important to know these tools exist so you can use them to make your meeting as rich and collaborative as it can be, there's no law that says you must *run* every meeting yourself. In fact, minding the minutiae of a web meeting can be a distraction that results in dead air, poor time management, and less-than-satisfactory outcomes.

Here's how those distractions impact us during a meeting. Imagine you're driving in an unfamiliar neighborhood, looking for an address. It's pouring down rain. What do you do? You turn down the radio so you can *see* better. It's natural; our brains can only handle so much stimulation, and we tend to shut off the functions that don't really matter. With web meetings, we often default to using as few tools as possible because we feel overwhelmed. That keeps the tool from being as useful as it could be.

Even if you know what your meeting should look like, and how to use the various functions to accomplish those goals, it can seem overwhelming to do all that clicking. Have someone else drive. That way you're free to actively listen, facilitate discussion, call on people as necessary, and remain focused on the task. Then someone else is responsible for making sure whatever's on the whiteboard is spelled correctly and that everyone can see the slides.

It's important that you understand the potential of the tools you have available and have an investment in (after all, you or someone in the organization is paying for them). You don't have to master the technology itself. It matters less who pushes the buttons than that your goals are achieved. A successful meeting won't happen, though, if the leader doesn't set a good example.

Show Up in Person

Just because we have ways to connect electronically doesn't mean we never again have to drive across town or hop on a plane. Consider questions like these: What are the circumstances when you should meet your team members? How often is it worth investing in that effort and expense? The dividends may well outweigh the direct cost/benefit analysis. Just because your team is remote doesn't mean you can't ever be face to face. Fight for the budget and resources to make it happen.

How to Get There

We have framed this chapter in terms of you as a leader and how and when you pick the tools to use. While all of that is true, we are talking about a team here. If you want technology to work most effectively for everyone, everyone needs to be involved in a conversation about it. Top-down edicts that declare "we're going to use this tool" generally encounter resistance. Invite your team to talk about which tools to use under what circumstances. From that conversation individuals can go find what works for them, and then the team can come together to find some common ground for rules or expectations about how and when technology is used. This way you'll get higher levels of engagement and adoption and there'll be less whining all around. Note: your job is to help get to the result, not do it all yourself.

Pause and Reflect

Ask yourself these questions:

▶ Which tools am I most comfortable with?

▶ Which tools am I least comfortable with?

▶ If I were to use them, how might they help add value to my communication efforts?

▶ What are some alternatives to "everyone at the same time" meetings?

▶ Who can I reach out to as a mentor, or teacher, to help me get better at using these tools?

Online Resources

If you want to have more effective conference calls, our checklist may help. Register at LongDistanceWorklife.com/Resources and request Conference Call Checklist.

If you want help with deciding which tools to use in your web meeting, register at LongDistanceWorklife.com/Resources and request the Virtual Presentation Checklist, or use this QR code to register for either tool.

Part IV Summary

So What?

- What is one area in which I've been engaging others well?

- What is one area in which I can improve the way I engage with others—especially those who are remote from me?

- How will the rise of hybrid work impact which tools I use?

Now What?

- What are specific action steps you can take to engage others more effectively?

- When will you begin?

- What help will you need?

- Where will you start?

Part V

Understanding Ourselves

It is not only the most difficult thing to know oneself,
but the most inconvenient one, too.

—Josh Billings, humorist and lecturer

Part V Introduction

How we lead ourselves in life impacts how we lead those around us.

—Michael Hyatt, entrepreneur and former CEO

We've talked about the focus of leadership: outcomes (where we are going) and others (the people who help us get there). Now we will talk about the core of leadership: ourselves. This is harder to talk about for several reasons:

- As humans we aren't very good at self-awareness.

- We all have egos, some of us overinflated, and others have less-than-stellar self-esteem.

- It is just uncomfortable. If you are wondering if this section is even necessary, we'll just say, yes, it is.

Let's dive in.

If you're a believer in servant leadership, you put yourself last, or at least behind other stakeholders. As we have shown, and as the 3O Model describes, we believe this is the only way we can lead. However, taken to the extreme, focusing on others can lead to sublimating yourself and to not taking care of your mental, physical, and social well-being. If you have vacation days piled up, or your spouse complains you are working while on the beach, you know what we mean.

If you're a command-and-control-type leader, the inability to always know what's going on can be frustrating and make you crazy. You try to constantly gather data, which interferes with people getting their work done. It is exhausting to try to keep up with every detail, and since no one wants to work for a micromanager, this approach also makes you a whole lot less fun to work with. There's an even tougher reality: remote workers who are unsatisfied are also unengaged and more prone to turnover.

Worst of all, if you are striving to be a servant leader and are fearful of exhibiting too much control, you may end up second-guessing yourself, and looking inconsistent, unclear, and indecisive.

Regardless of the kind of leader you are, or aspire to be, you can't really focus on the desired outcomes, or engage with your team, without looking at the one constant—yourself. A leader who is physically exhausted, mentally drained, and socially isolated is not going to be effective.

We need to be honest about how we're doing and take care of ourselves. While we are generally not the first people you would associate with Oprah, we do adhere to one of her core precepts: you can't take care of others if you don't take care of yourself first. If you're stressed and drained physically, spiritually, and mentally, and lack self-awareness of how you are impacting others, you can't be an effective leader, no matter where you and your team work.

What you have read in this introduction so far is straight from the first edition of the book. We felt we needed to clarify and make these points. They are still important—but hopefully we don't have to sell you as much as we did in 2018. If you lived and led through the pandemic, you know what we're talking about. The question is, have you done (or are you continuing to do) anything about it? And what will you do going forward with what you have learned?

This is the shortest section of the book, but don't misunderstand—it is as important as any of the others. If you want to lead more effectively, you must live more effectively.

Chapter 14

Getting Honest Feedback

Rule 14: Seek feedback to best serve outcomes, others, and ourselves.

We all need people who will give us feedback. That's how we improve.
—Bill Gates, former CEO of Microsoft

Nicole wanted to be an effective leader. She worked hard trying to keep up with the latest leadership practices. But all that effort sometimes left her frustrated and confused. She wanted to know more than just what to do; she wanted to know how she was doing. At the end of the day, she didn't have a clear picture of how successful she was. This left her more than frustrated; it severely hampered her confidence, too.

When you work apart from those you lead, you typically lack the instantaneous feedback you need to function at a high level. As leaders, if we don't get regular, honest feedback from our people, it's easy to get excited about the wrong things, remain unaware of our blind spots, or ignore inconvenient facts. This can lead to everything from repeating mistakes, to seeming foolish, to making decisions that are doomed to fail. How many requests have you made of people that you would have changed or avoided if you could've seen the terrified look on their faces? In the conference room, or on the shop floor, you would see that look—but over the phone, in an email, or in an instant message, not so much. In today's world of work, how do you get that feedback and those insights?

Generating Ideas

While estimates vary, we have between twenty-five and thirty thoughts every minute. Some are valuable ("We should update our branding.") some are musings that may lead nowhere ("What would happen if we opened a Denver office?") and many are questionable ("Handlebar mustaches are cool, right?"). To sort these ideas and decide which to proceed with, we need feedback.

Wayne once worked for someone he respected greatly. He also feared every time she came to the office from out of town because a lot of her conversations began with "So, I was reading this article on the plane . . ."

Inevitably, she would have read something that got her thinking on her transcontinental flight. She noodled the idea over and over, playing out different "what if" scenarios in her mind. Being a positive person, she began to see the possibilities and even began to think about implementation, results, and what success would look like. By the time she arrived in the regional office, she was bubbling with enthusiasm for the plan and asking people to get to work on it.

The problem was there were always new plans, and while some of them were excellent, even more contradicted previous priorities or initiatives, or had consequences she hadn't considered. Since saying "For the love of all that's holy, stop reading on airplanes!" was a nonstarter, Wayne had to step up and say, "Can we stop and think about this for a moment?" Often the ideas were killed or at least scaled back to something manageable. It helped that she was reasonable and open to that kind of feedback.

We aren't suggesting you stop thinking or being enthusiastic about your ideas. You must remember, though, to share and gain feedback on the ideas before you unilaterally decree action that might scare, alienate, or confuse your team.

Listening to the Right Voices

Of course, it's not simply the positive, action-oriented, idea-generating voices in your head that get your attention. You are also at the mercy of negative self-talk and pessimism that can demotivate or immobilize you. When we can get out of our own head, and still listen to the ideas of others, we can get past the negative thinking. The more you work alone, the harder it is to get that interaction.

When your team is remote, it always takes effort to talk with them. As we've said, too often the conversations become transactional and to the point. It is bad enough that leaders don't always ask for feedback—and even more often team members are reluctant to offer it—but this dynamic is made worse at a distance. Additionally, there is a difference between being alone and being lonely. Scientists tell us that being alone with our thoughts is good and helpful; we need time to think, daydream, relax, and refresh. Prolonged isolation, though, can seriously impact our behavior, mood, and even health. Even the most introverted among us requires some social interaction. This isolation, as we have mentioned several times in the book, needs to be a real concern for you (not just your team members). You must be vigilant and intentional in asking for feedback, not just on your ideas, but also on how you are doing overall.

Finally, as a reminder: the dark side of being a dedicated, caring leader is that it's easy to diminish your own needs to the point that you care so much about everyone else, you don't take proper care of yourself.

Data versus Context

It's important to understand that information comes in two forms: data and context.

Data is relatively easy to get. How many units did we sell last month? Do customers like our latest offering? What does our retention look like? These questions can be answered with numbers, and it is likely you and your team can access that information no matter where you work.

Context, on the other hand, adds perspective and translates the raw data into actual, useful information you can act on. For example, if you sold 2,500 widgets this month but normally sell 1,000, that's good news. If 5,000 is a normal month, there's a problem. Still, it's essentially one set of data compared to another set of data; the context is just different. How do your people feel about that? Are they motivated and excited, or discouraged and uninspired? The actions you take and the way you communicate can vary greatly depending on their reactions.

Soliciting feedback can help you communicate and lead far more effectively.

Was your speech intended to inspire them, lighting a fire, or scorch them, reducing their motivation to ashes? Before sending out that email or calling that town hall meeting, you need to check your assumptions. How we process and respond to both the data and the context determines our actions, and the actions of those we lead. But where does a leader gain that context? It usually comes through feedback of one sort or another.

As we've said, when you walk the plant floor, or stand in the middle of the cubicle farm where people are working, you can sense the mood of the team. When you sit miles away from most or all of your team, you're drawing conclusions based on how you feel about the situation, or what you've seen in a few email threads or heard in one quick conversation with a team member. Soliciting feedback can help you communicate and lead far more effectively.

Soliciting Information and Feedback

A natural reaction when faced with a challenge is to find a small number of people you trust and ask, "What do you think?" That's a good start, yet it may not be enough. Remember the inherent power imbalance. If you hold positional authority over people, their answers may be tentative, incomplete, or simply what they think you want to hear.

The TV show *Undercover Boss* demonstrated this beautifully (if a little painfully for those of us in positions of authority). The CEO of a company would wear a disguise and go out among rank-and-file employees in the business to see how things were really operating, and to solicit feedback about their performance without the barrier of positional authority. Whether the news was good or bad, the leaders were always surprised by what they learned, and they were concerned about the gap between their perception of what was happening and the reality of work. While there were some brand awareness advantages for being on the show, fundamentally, these CEOs went to tremendous effort to get feedback that they couldn't or didn't get otherwise.

This isn't a new concept. *Arabian Nights* tells of wise sultans who went out in disguise at night to see what was really happening in their cities. The lessons are the same: no matter how benevolent and beloved you are, or think you are, as a leader, getting honest feedback is complicated and difficult. Yet how else can you check your assumptions, evaluate decisions more effectively, and lead most effectively in support of both outcomes and others?

When soliciting feedback on yourself, especially as a leader, keep some things in mind:

- *Start with existing evidence.* Before going to individuals, go back through relevant files, email threads, and meeting notes. Ask yourself, how are people feeling? What are they thinking about how I'm doing, the way I'm interacting, and the decisions I'm making?

- *Identify people you trust.* Don't confuse this with people you like or who always say yes to your ideas. Trusted advisors can come from many sources: people you know will tell you the truth as they see it regardless of your position, those who care about you and your success, coworkers with technical expertise that you don't possess, and anyone with first-hand information about the other stakeholders such as employees, customers, or partners. *Note: If this list of people, especially on your own team, is small, you have a problem! Review the Trust Triangle and get honest with yourself to see why this might be.*

- *Ask open-ended questions.* Remember that no matter how sincere your quest may be, you're still the boss asking, "Do you think this will work?" Since you're asking, the assumption is that you think it will, or if you're scowling about it, they know you're skeptical and they probably should be too. A better way to ask is "Based on what you've heard, what about this would work? What would be a problem? How do you think people will respond (and why)?" Make the questions truly open and not presumptive or leading.

- *Use the PIN technique when seeking feedback.* PIN stands for positive, interesting, and negative. By using this technique yourself, and encouraging those around you to use it, there's a good chance you'll get more honest answers and be more able to accept what you receive.

  - *Positive.* Describe what is good or valuable about the idea, situation, or behavior. When you start positive, defenses don't immediately go up. This makes the conversation more effective and agreement more likely.

  - *Interesting.* Since the situation or idea might be complex, discuss it a bit further. This is often where trust can be built in the feedback conversation. Discussing what's interesting is a neutral way of identifying things we don't know or assumptions people have.

  - *Negative.* Share the objections, concerns, and negative consequences of the idea, action, or behavior. Once the positive aspects have been acknowledged, people are more willing to listen to objections or roadblocks.

  This technique works best when used consistently and modeled constantly. When you regularly respond to questions this way, over time this will be the way your team communicates with you and each other.

- *Have these conversations as richly as possible.* When communicating with people over the phone, you can't see the gleam in their eyes or if they are rolling them as you speak. If you try to elicit a response via email or instant messages, the value and clarity of the information you receive may be reduced (and in an email, it is easier for people to respond with just "fine" or "it's good"). If you really want feedback and input, take the time and use the tools in the ways we've discussed. Schedule the conversation, block in sufficient time, and use the tools at your disposal. Use your webcams and meeting tools when possible.

- *Make these conversations ongoing.* If what you're considering is really important, know that people may do their best thinking before and after the conversation. If you want good insight, make sure people prepare for the conversation (fly-by requests, whether in their office or online, don't always result in deep thinking because their minds are busy thinking about something else). These conversations should happen in an honest and candid way. How often have we hung up the phone only to realize there was something we hadn't thought of, or something we should have phrased another way? Using asynchronous methods like email (or better, shared folders or documents that people can update at any time and easily refer to) will allow people to add value to their original thoughts. This also gives you the chance to go over them again and reevaluate the feedback when you're calm and ready to think more rationally.

One of the best ways to build your self-awareness as a leader is with a 360 Assessment. This is a way to gather anonymous feedback from your team, your peers, and your boss(es), and it can include outside stakeholders like customers and suppliers. Many organizations already do this as part of the performance review process or at other times. There are a couple of caveats when using these tools:

- The feedback must be anonymous.

- The data is only as good as the questions you ask.

For this reason, many leaders and organizations turn to outside parties to conduct these assessments. We offer this service, but so do hundreds of other capable consultants and organizations. We believe the process and coaching that goes with this process is more important than the survey itself—not because the questions don't matter, but because there are plenty of good instruments. The process can seem time-consuming, but like the sultan and many Undercover Bosses have found, the results can be eye-opening.

Pause and Reflect

Ask yourself these questions:

- ▶ Am I getting enough feedback from others?
- ▶ How confident am I in the quality of that feedback?
- ▶ Do I regularly ask for it?
- ▶ Who will give me honest feedback?
- ▶ How open am I to feedback?

Chapter 15

Your Beliefs and Self-Talk

**Evidence is conclusive that your self-talk has a
direct bearing on your performance.**

—Zig Ziglar, speaker and author

Nathan had been a successful individual contributor and was promoted to leadership. While he doubted his skills, he was leading people who were doing work he had done, so he felt he was doing a good job overall. Senior leaders thought he was doing better than that—they promoted him again. Now he finds himself leading people in three countries doing work he's never done. He lies awake at night wondering if he's really up to the challenge, and he is sure he'll be exposed as unqualified for his job. He wonders if he can ever succeed in this situation.

Good leaders require a relatively healthy self-image. After all, if you don't think you are correct a good percentage of the time, that you're somewhat capable, or the right person for the job, you likely won't find yourself in this position. Unless you are a complete sociopath, the voices in your head aren't always supportive or positive.

Remember the Walt Disney movie *Pinocchio*? One of the heroic characters in that movie was Jiminy Cricket. Although he often sounded like a stick-in-the-mud and a drag, he was there to remind Pinocchio that if he engaged in certain behavior, he'd never become a real boy. Sometimes Pinocchio listened, often he didn't, but at least he wasn't working solely on the unchecked whims of his wooden heart.

In essence, Jiminy was an *auriga*. The auriga was a servant of the Roman Emperor, whose job, according to legend, was to stand behind the emperor during large public events and whisper, *memento homo*—"remember, you are just a man"—so that the love of the crowd and the celebration of power wouldn't go to the emperor's head. It didn't make them popular, but the job was valuable.

What we believe about ourselves dictates how successful we will be.

What if the auriga was a totally negative downer, saying things like, "You're an idiot, nobody likes you," instead of providing a healthy and necessary warning, "Are you sure you want to do that?" How motivated would Caesar have been to make the tough decisions or implement any kind of change? Too much pessimistic programming would have changed how he led and drastically changed his results.

What we believe about ourselves dictates how successful we will be. And our beliefs are formed and reinforced by how we talk to ourselves. Asking ourselves questions and checking our assumptions is natural and necessary. Running ourselves down and focusing on the negative is terribly destructive. The good news about talking to yourself is that you can change the conversation at any time.

Here are some warning signs that your internal dialogue is going in an unhealthy direction and how to steer it onto a more positive path:

- *"You're an idiot. That's the worst idea ever."* Really? *Ever?* At times like this, it's okay to revert to middle school and ask yourself, "Says who?" If you take that question seriously, it takes you back to the neutral facts. What evidence is there to support or deny your idea or premise? You might be wrong; it's highly unlikely you're an idiot. And it's even more certain it's not the worst idea ever.

- *"I can't do this."* The words we use matter. *Can't* is a statement of fact. It cannot be done—it defies the natural laws of the physical world. (I truly *cannot* lift an elephant with my bare hands.) To say, "I can't hit you with a shovel," is probably not true, but it might not be a good idea. When you get frustrated to the point of saying you can't do something, change the word. "I haven't yet figured out how to . . ." or "Up until now I haven't been able to do it" are different ideas entirely. When you change the wording, you recognize that you have difficulties, but you still accept the possibility of success, which changes your internal motivation. It also suggests you might need help from elsewhere. Maybe the problem you're trying to solve requires a different solution, but when you are stuck in "I can't," it is hard to see that. You absolutely cannot lift an elephant with your bare hands, but if an elevated pachyderm is what you want, the nearby rope and pulleys might be of assistance. Just because the way you are trying to accomplish something doesn't work doesn't mean the goal is unattainable. It just means you need to stop doing what you're doing and take another look. The same goes for words like *won't*, *never*, and *impossible.*

- *"I'm a fraud and I will be exposed."* This feeling, known as *impostor syndrome,* is estimated to affect over 70 percent of leaders.[1] Here are some simple techniques to help address this monster:

- *Check your assumptions.* Recognize your "I can'ts" for what they are. When in doubt, ask, "Says who?"

- *Accept positive feedback as valid.* When people tell you how smart or capable you are, believe them and don't dismiss or downplay it. Why would they say it if they didn't see something positive?

- *Get help.* Remember that the best and brightest go to others for help, feedback, and answers.

- *Consider past success.* You've had success in the past; you will have more in the future. Think back to a similar challenge and how you addressed that.

- *Treat yourself like you would any other competent person.* Don't accept feedback from yourself you wouldn't offer to anyone else. Would you call someone else "totally useless?" Probably not because it would only make things worse and not address the real problem. Are you different from anyone else?

- *"I've just been lucky so far."* Las Vegas is built on one simple premise: luck only gets you so far, and there's really no such thing. Don't denigrate your past performance or successes.

When you notice you are mired in this negative self-talk, a break may help. Take a walk or indulge in some menial chore that doesn't take too much brain power. Take time to reflect on your past successes and ask yourself positive questions. The PIN technique described in the last chapter works for us as well as with others. Why treat other people better than you treat yourself?

Another simple way to address self-talk is to stop talking to yourself and talk to other humans. Schedule a coaching call with an employee. Touch base with former colleagues who will probably remind you what a rockstar you were when you worked together. Call your mom—hearing a voice that's happy to hear yours is an instant pick-me-up.

It takes a conscious effort to reach out to other people, especially when you're wallowing in negativity, but even the most casual social interaction gets you out of your own head and allows you to replenish your courage and self-worth.

Why do we share this chapter? Because if you are working alone your self-talk can become even louder and you have no mitigating voices to offer positive feedback. Listen to the way you speak to yourself and make sure it is serving you, your results, and your team. If it isn't, remember that even if it takes time and practice, you can change it.

Pause and Reflect

Ask yourself these questions:

▶ What are my beliefs about myself as a leader?

▶ How are my beliefs about myself helping or hindering my progress and success?

▶ How often does negative self-talk interfere with my confidence or decision making?

▶ When I am caught in a cycle of negative self-talk, what's one thing I can do immediately to refocus my energy in a positive way?

Chapter 16

Setting Clear Boundaries

Rule 16: Setting clear boundaries is necessary for you to be an effective Long-Distance Leader.

Boundaries are, in simple terms, the recognition of personal space.

—Asa Don Brown, author and clinical psychologist

Lousia began as a leader during the pandemic in a fully remote setting. As the lockdowns ended, her organization moved to a hybrid model, but she is still only in the office two days a week. She aspired to lead and has high expectations for herself. She finds the job hard. She is often exhausted and her family feels like she isn't present with them much of the time. If she is honest with herself, they are right. But she doesn't know how to change things in a way that meets her team's needs, her family's needs, and her career desires.

If you detach from Lousia's story it is easy to say she needs to set some boundaries. But if you see yourself in her story, you know it's easier said than done.

Ultimately, only you can look at your work and life and decide what boundaries you need to set.

Boundaries are the limits and rules we set for ourselves and with others. They define and describe how and when we will interact and in what ways. At work we often talk about expectations, and we certainly do in this book. The boundaries we set for ourselves as leaders and human beings can end up being connected to some expectations, and once we set them, they might cause expectations to change.

How Boundaries Help Us

When we intentionally set boundaries we care about, they can help us in a variety of ways. Boundaries can

- *Reduce decision fatigue.* Once you have decided how you will handle a situation, you don't have to think about it—just follow the rule you set for yourself.

- *Create successful habits.* We all have plenty of habits. Setting clear boundaries is the precursor to creating more good habits in your life. After all, you wouldn't set a boundary that makes things worse for yourself, would you?

- *Clarify expectations.* For example, if you set a boundary about when you stop working for the day, you help others understand how to work with you most effectively—and as a leader, you can model the behavior you expect from your team.

- *Reduce stress.* Clear boundaries around response times and workload management can significantly reduce stress. Your boundaries can help you disconnect and reduce the feeling of constant pressure.

- *Enhance focus.* With less stress and decision fatigue, you will be able to focus more clearly and productively.

- *Increase credibility and build trust.* When you set and respect boundaries, you set a good example and gain respect for your discipline and clarity.

- *Enhance relationships.* Boundaries help create healthier interpersonal relationships—both at home and at work. They build trust, help set priorities, and reduce misunderstandings and conflicts.

- *Improve work/life balance.* Nearly any work-related boundaries you set will likely help you put your life in better balance, further reducing stress, increasing your happiness, and improving your relationships.

This is a good list, but setting boundaries only helps us if we live within them. That means we must dedicate ourselves to these boundaries and share them with the relevant people around us. For some, that means our teammates. For others, it may mean our family. Anyone who is affected by (and hopefully will benefit from) boundaries needs to know, and when they do, they can help us be accountable to living up to those decisions.

Some Boundaries to Consider

Ultimately, only you can look at your work and life and decide what boundaries you need to set. We hope you will consider the list that follows. We have coached and trained hundreds of leaders for whom some of these were gamechangers. We've personally experienced their power as well. As you read the list, think about your situation and how a boundary in these areas could serve you and those around you.

- *Working hours.* When will you work, and when will you shut down? This was (a little) easier when you had to pack up from the office and head home, but especially on the days you work from home, when will you stop? And before you answer, think about how your answer impacts your team. Maybe you are an empty-nester, or young and single and want to work more, but remember your model is a message to the rest of the team. Make sure your boundary is workable for the rest of the team too.

- *Weekends.* Will you work on weekends, and if so, under what circumstances?

- *Vacation.* What are your work boundaries when you are on vacation? Kevin knows the struggle between being available if needed and being present with those you are vacationing with. Remember that being available (except in extreme emergencies) keeps the team from developing and doesn't give them the sense that you trust them. If you work internationally, recognize that the average American does not take or use all their vacation and personal time, whereas in other countries it is illegal to expect people to give up their allotted personal time.

- *Email and messaging hours.* When are you looking at and sending emails? Remember if you are sending emails at night and on weekends, people are likely to read them, even if they don't respond. If you need or want to send emails at night or on the weekend, we strongly advise that you learn how to delay the delivery until others are back at work. (The same holds true for emails to people when they are on vacation, whenever possible.)

- *Response times.* What will your response times be for emails? For instant messages? For return calls? And "immediately" isn't necessary or helpful. Your answers here will relate to your boundaries on the items earlier on the list.

- *Meeting schedules.* Some organizations have banned meetings on a certain day or during times of the day. What are your boundaries for numbers of, times of, and lengths of meetings? We know that you don't schedule all the meetings, but you also don't have to automatically attend every meeting you are invited to. Your boundaries here can help you create a more productive working day and might help you reduce the meeting fatigue of your team too.

- *Communication channels.* We've talked in an earlier chapter about which tools are best for which types of communications. Here we are talking about which is the tool you might check in emergencies. Is there one way people could reach you if needed while you are on vacation? Which tool will family members always use to get your attention during the workday? Answers to these questions help everybody— perhaps more than you realize.

- *Digital detox.* When do you (or do you?) unplug and put down your devices? Whether it is all weekend, once a month, or something else, this is a question worth considering. Your example matters more to your team than you might realize.

- *Personal interruptions.* If you are working at home, when and how can others interrupt you—and what is a valid reason for interruptions? Your answer will vary with your situation (and perhaps the age of your kids), but boundaries here can help you honor everyone and all your commitments more effectively.

- *Personal activities.* What activities take priority for you? You probably know someone who never misses a kid's game or recital and someone else who never makes one. Who do you want to be? You can decide and set a boundary and improve your success, whatever your right answer is.

- *Where you work.* We know you work at your desk and at home. But we mean more than that. Do you have a space at home where you work?

And places where you don't? Is the laptop on the couch okay for you or not?

- *Physical activity.* You can decide about your breaks and your physical activity. If you are a runner or gym-goer, is that time nonnegotiable as a boundary? If not, chances are your success and consistency is lower.

Now that you have looked at this list, which of these areas are most important to you?

Pause and Reflect

Ask yourself these questions:

- ▶ What boundaries do I have now?
- ▶ Are they adequate and helpful?
- ▶ What other boundaries could I set?
- ▶ Who could I ask for input on them?

Chapter 17

Setting Personal Priorities

Rule 17: Balance your priorities to be a Remarkable Long-Distance Leader.

I learned that we can do anything, but we can't do everything . . . at least not at the same time. So think of your priorities not in terms of what activities you do, but when you do them. Timing is everything.

—Dan Millman, author

Donald is an experienced sales manager who has worked hard to become VP of international sales. He finds the work exhilarating, and he's proud of reaching his career goals. Since his children have grown and moved out of the house, he should have plenty of time to get his work done without distractions. Yet, he doesn't feel as good as he should. Physically, he's worn out and now, at the busiest time of the year, he finds himself listless and not as enthusiastic as he knows he needs to be. His team is complaining that he's working them too hard and isn't really listening to their concerns. A new mandate that everyone must go into the office twice a week feels *unnecessary since they actually raised their productivity when working from home. This has caused resentment and frustration. He has altered vacation plans twice, and his wife is no happier than his team members. This should be the high point of his career, but it sure doesn't feel like it.*

If you are still reading, we are confident that you think of yourself last. As we talked about throughout the book, Outcomes and Others do come before Ourselves. That doesn't mean we surrender our humanity, our health, or our sanity. There is a difference between self-preservation and selfishness.

Let's start with values. Your values determine how you decide what is truly important to you. Our goal isn't to suggest what your values are but rather to urge *you* to be clear on what they are.

So, what is important to you?

When you ask questions about what is important to you, and answer honestly, you will begin to see that the barriers to managing your time are mostly of your own construction. Everyone has the same amount of time—the question is how to use it. As Kevin says in *Remarkable Leadership*, time management is really *choice* management. If you aren't clear on your values, you can't make clear choices on how to use your time.

The challenges of hybrid work can also complicate things. When you allow your people to use their time more flexibly, or time zones play a larger role in the team's work, you can feel more pressure than ever.

There is a difference between self-preservation and selfishness.

Knowing your values allows you to prioritize your activities. For example, if you need spiritual balance, working on the finance reports on Sunday might be a bad call. If you need physical exercise to be happy and productive, go to the gym—that time to yourself won't undo all your good work for the week.

We aren't saying making changes to regain control will be easy. First, you need to help people understand how best to work with you. As a simple example, if your email inbox has become unmanageable, encourage people to help you prioritize your messages. When they absolutely need you to read and respond, they should put you on the "To" line. When they are merely keeping you in the loop or don't need you to act immediately, tell them to put your name on the "Cc" line instead. This will help you spend your time on things that matter, and people won't expect you to respond to everything they send.

Even though this is about you, you'll need help and support to make these changes. Ask people you trust to help you manage your time. Most will be happy to help. If you need an accountability partner, find one. If your goal is to stop answering email in the middle of the night, have someone you trust call you on it. When they remind you that the email saying "thanks" went out at 2:00 a.m., it will bring you back to your senses.

If you haven't yet, make a list of things that are important to you, and ask yourself: "Am I satisfied with the time I'm giving to each activity and person on my list?" If the answer is no, try to identify small blocks of time you can dedicate to each. These are some typical items on the list:

- Physical exercise

- My spouse

- The kids' bedtime (or ball game, recital, or other activities)

- Spiritual practices

- Friends

- Reading and self-development

- A hobby

Hobbies and unstructured leisure time are more important than you think. Activities that take your brain away from work will often spark some of your best thinking and make you happier and easier to live with. If Albanian klezmer music is your thing, go to a concert. Join a band. Turn your phone off in the car and crank your tunes until you feel better. What you do with this time doesn't need to make sense to anyone else. Kevin's obsessed with antique

John Deere tractors. Seriously, it's a thing. He goes to auctions and slows down when he sees anything green in a field. The team teases him about it, but it makes him a happier and more well-rounded person. Whatever floats your boat matters. Take it seriously.

Take advantage of asynchronous work so that you are not spending time on meetings that can be handled in other ways. Kevin has his sales team do a short, written report each week; the salesperson can write the report at their convenience and put it in a Slack channel. Then he can look at it when he's ready. This has reduced the time he (and the team) spends on meetings and shortens conversations because so much information has already been shared.

None of this is new information to you, and we don't want to sound trite. But just because you've heard it before doesn't mean you're comfortable guarding your personal time and energy. If you were, you'd already have greater balance and be less stressed. You have to give yourself the same permission to engage with yourself you'd allow any member of your team. Take it as seriously as you do when you engage with the organization and others, and for all the same reasons.

Pause and Reflect

Ask yourself these questions:

▶ What is my proudest current accomplishment as a leader?

▶ What is one thing in my personal life I am proud of that doesn't involve my work?

▶ What is one thing in my personal life that should be getting more of my time than I'm currently allotting?

Part VI

Developing
Long-Distance Leaders

**Growing other leaders from the ranks isn't just the
duty of the leader, it's an obligation.**

—Warren Bennis, author and consultant

Chapter 18

Questions to Ask about Developing Long-Distance Leaders

Rule 18: Ensure your leadership development prepares Long-Distance Leaders.

The growth and development of people is the highest calling of leadership.
—Harvey Firestone, American businessman

Audrey is in the training department at an international tech company. She's struggling with a paradox. On the one hand, she has requests from individual leaders and managers who are adjusting to the differences in leading people who aren't in their location. On the other hand, senior management is shrinking training budgets and wondering why the current leadership development efforts aren't more effective. Audrey's wondering if they need to scrap their entire legacy leadership training or whether they can find a way to adjust their current efforts without reinventing the wheel.

At the beginning of the book, we promised assistance for those of you responsible for developing Long-Distance Leaders in your organizations. Whether you are an individual manager trying to grow the leadership capabilities of your team, or you're in charge of learning and development for a huge corporation, we want to share some additional strategies and approaches to create a plan for growing great leaders in the dispersed and hybrid workplace.

When considering leadership development, we believe three pairs of questions need to be considered:

- What kind of organization do you want to be? / Does your current culture match this vision?

- What behaviors do you expect from your Long-Distance Leaders? / What skill gaps exist?

- What is your plan for developing and supporting your Long-Distance Leaders? / How will the organization support remote team members?

Let's explore each of these in detail.

What Kind of Organization Do You Want to Be? Does Your Current Culture Match This Vision?

Having a clear picture of how a remote workforce fits into the culture you want to create is important. What your remote or hybrid situation looks like has changed and will continue to evolve. Hybrid work may be just a compromise way of working that will change over time. We encourage you to step back and think about how remote and hybrid work will impact and inform your organizational culture now and in the future.

We define *culture* as "the way we do things here." That means every organization and every team has one. It doesn't take much insight to realize that when people work apart from each other, the way things are really done can vary greatly from the culture you think (or hope) you have.

So, you have a culture—but it may not have developed intentionally or be the one you want. In a remote and dispersed workplace, if you don't define and assess the culture you want, you may wind up with something completely unintended. To take a deeper dive into this crucial topic, we recommend you check out *The Long-Distance Team: Designing Your Team for Everyone's Success*.

Descriptions of the organization, such as "we don't depend much on titles here," are obvious when the CEO parks and walks as far in the rain as everyone else. But if you work from home and have never seen the soaked CEO, you may not believe that titles don't matter and be unduly stressed when you get a request from her. Organizations need to be intentional and consistent in how they communicate, or they won't reinforce the culture they aspire to.

Since working in these new ways has never happened before in the history of business, it's logical that there will be successes and failures. There is no magic bullet.

After the pandemic, many companies immediately tried to get back to normal by mandating that everyone return to the office. Some reasons were solid (teams didn't seem to brainstorm or collaborate as effectively as they used to). Other reasons were less so. A lot of leaders hated seeing space they were paying for sit unoccupied.

Some of these concerns were valid, but leaders ignored other factors. For instance, individual task completion can rise in remote environments, and work/life balance can enhance employee satisfaction and engagement.

As the pandemic lessened in severity, Google was one company that let everyone continue to work from home if they wished, but then they changed their minds and insisted on more time in-office. This created a backlash that led to grumbling and resignations.

Without guidance, people working remotely and left to their own devices tend to become very task-focused and independent. If that is what you are looking for from your people, having them remain or become remote-first is the right answer. Good examples include a team of individual customer service reps or salespeople who are focused on their quotas. Google assumed finding the right balance of remote and in-person work would happen organically—give smart people the mission and the tools and they'll figure it out—but that's not what happened.

You could argue that Google overreacted, yet similar changes have occurred at Yahoo, Apple, and other companies who implemented remote working without thinking through the consequences. They didn't anticipate how remote work would impact the team, and then the result of pulling those people back to the office. If things weren't working, it was appropriate to reexamine the decision and make a change. But these situations aren't an indictment on the potential of remote or hybrid work, nor do they indicate a shift away from it. Many companies that were completely co-located have since gone hybrid. Some have arrived at their version of a hybrid model through deliberate and mindful planning. But too often it has been a knee-jerk response to changing employee demands. "If we make them come back into the office, they'll quit, so we'll only call them in a couple of days a week." That's a compromise, not a strategy. As long as senior leaders feel they "lost," they will look for chances to change the agreement as conditions change. We strongly suggest a deliberate approach based on the needs of the work, not based solely on the whims and wishes of leaders and the team.

Leading remotely means you may need to add to or at least address certain skills and knowledge in your current learning offerings.

Your cultural aspirations need to be supported by processes. For example, if using the technology available to build strong remote teams is critical to managing your project, is that supported by your performance review? If your leaders are assessed on their communication skills, are they held accountable for their ability to effectively use the tools at their disposal? If contributing to team brainstorms and discussions is a core competency for team members, are they coached on their lack of contribution to virtual meetings or conference calls? Or are people simply allowed to log on, answer email, and claim they were there?

Peter Drucker said, "Put good people in a bad system, and the system wins every time." Intentionally developing a culture means not only educating and empowering leaders, but also having the whole organization work in concert to achieve desired behaviors. Here are two examples of parts of the organization that need to be aligned:

- *Human Resources.* Do your organization's performance management systems reflect the reality of how people work today? Do your support systems, like the learning management system and annual performance reviews, reflect the additional skills and changed dynamics of leading people and working together from a distance? Are the processes for assessing, rewarding, and promoting teleworkers equal to those for people in the office?

- *Information Technology.* Do your IT people make all the technology decisions and provide the training? If so, you may have created unintended cultural problems. For example, if they're continually concerned about VPN bandwidth, they may decree that nobody can use webcams. Do you want that decision made in a vacuum, or do you want a real conversation that considers the culture you want and the real world expectations of your leaders before that decision is made?

Too many organizations have placed limits on what their people can and can't do based on either old thinking or faulty assumptions about what their jobs really entail. During the pandemic, the need to limit the growing number of collaboration and meeting tools forced companies to try to find unified solutions. This led to organizations choosing Microsoft Teams over other tools.

At the beginning, several features that learning and development needed weren't present in Teams, but the decision to implement Teams (and other tools) was made without consulting many of the people who would use them every day. Had there been more consultation and contributions from end users, problems like this could have been avoided.

What Behaviors Do You Expect from Your Long-Distance Leaders? What Skill Gaps Exist?

We recommend using your existing leadership competences as your starting point, then using all three gears in the Remote Leadership Model (refer to Figure 4 in Chapter 4) to frame the discussion about additions or changes driven by leading remotely. Here is some help for those conversations.

Leadership and Management

Compare your leadership competency list with the ideas we have talked about in the book. Ask yourself:

- Does our existing competency model accurately reflect the expectations we have of our remote leaders?

- If not, what isn't addressed?

- Do we need to be more explicit or specific on any of the competencies for Long-Distance Leaders?

When you lead remotely, you may need to add certain skills and knowledge, or at least address them in your current learning offerings. Before you say, "Yes, we have coaching and communication workshops," think about the nuances that will lead you to success in this new working environment in areas like coaching, delegating, communicating, leading meetings, building relationships, setting goals, and more. Leaders need to be aware of both the differences in dynamics between working remotely and in the office and specific techniques to help address and mitigate those differences.

Hybrid work raises issues that may have been under the surface but are now evident. Proximity bias is a classic example.

Remember Rule #1—leadership first, location second. Yes, you may have the core competencies covered in your leadership development offerings, but do they address the nuances you need today? If you have specifically thought about and addressed this question, the chances are they don't.

If these learning opportunities aren't already available to your leaders, they should be, and in a variety of methodologies. This includes the traditional classroom environment, virtual training, e-learning, self-paced instruction, and likely blended learning processes that include several components.

Tools and Technology

This gear most directly impacts how leaders make the shift from traditional leadership to leading in a remote or virtual environment. Consider these questions to clarify your organizational expectations of your Long-Distance Leaders.

- Which tools do we want them to use, and when should they use them? This is the richness versus scope discussion. Do people know how to use Teams/Webex/Slack or whatever tools you employ? And by *use*, we mean they know more than how to open the application. Provide expectations and guidance for them based on our recommendations in this book.

- What does "use the tools effectively" look like? This includes helping them learn the mechanics of the tools (do they know which button to push?) and also helping them use the technology to facilitate an engaging, interactive, and effective meeting (which is as much about facilitation and leadership as it is about technology).

Skills and Impact

The smallest gear in the model shows that all your good intentions and expensive technology don't matter if you don't use your tools effectively.

- Do they use the tools in an effective way? It is important to understand what leaders need to do and what tools they have at their disposal *and* also be aware that they need to use those tools well. If leaders don't feel confident using technology, they won't be nearly as effective as they should be.

■ Do people have the chance to practice? People need to practice and receive coaching and feedback when the pressure isn't on. You won't solve this confidence gap with the online tutorials that came with your software license. Assuming these out-of-the-box tutorials will get the job done is one reason organizations don't get maximum return on their technology investment.

What Is Your Plan for Developing and Supporting Our Long-Distance Leaders?
How Will the Organization Support the Remote Team Members?

When you have answers to all the preceding questions, you are prepared to create a plan to develop your Long-Distance Leaders. Too often there isn't a real plan; rather, someone makes a decision to "add a course," or "send some people" to a training class without context and a clear purpose for those attending or for the entire organization.

Notice we didn't include the word *training* in the question. That was intentional. We believe the focus of "developing and supporting" should be *learning* and not simply training. When you change your perspective to learning you will do three things:

■ *Connect learning to the work.* We are sometimes asked to travel to organizations and teach people how to lead teams remotely. While we can do that, it doesn't make much sense. Can you teach people how to effectively communicate using technology if you are not using the technology? Seeing these tools used in the context of actual work is a powerful learning experience. Otherwise, it is like teaching people to swim in a gym. Learning happens fastest and best when it is directly related to the work people do, in the way they do it. It also needs to be realistic: Does the training reflect how people will work? If certain jobs need to be done in the office, do the training there. If people are remote, take that into account. Here's another (too common) example: during a workshop, encouraging people to collaborate and work together is a lost cause if all their key performance indicators (KPIs) are individually focused.

- *Make learning available in different ways.* If your workplace is a complex mixture of people working in all sorts of locations, in different time zones, and with different work schedules, shouldn't the ways they learn the related skills reflect this reality? Make sure you have a mix of both asynchronous and synchronous options available to your remote leaders and their teams.

- *Make it a process.* We believe that training is an event, but learning is a process. If you want people to transfer what they are learning to the workplace, change a habit, and build confidence in doing new things, an event alone will always fall short. *No one learned to play a piano well by attending a piano skills workshop.* We learn skills over time, not all at once. Coaching (one-on-one or group) and mentoring can and should be included in your leadership development plans.

Although we are admittedly biased, we believe that while you don't want to outsource everything we have just described, you probably also don't want to do it all internally. The nuances in skills and the context of working with people remotely are different than what your training department is likely used to delivering.

Finally, if your IT is tasked with teaching the technology tools, be aware of these possible problems:

- *It takes more than a demonstration.* To teach a technology effectively requires context, demonstration, application, and ongoing coaching. Simply recording someone who is proficient in the technology (but not in facilitating learning) and making the recording available is not training. Do your IT people have the resources and expertise to help people really learn these skills?

- *IT is focused on the tool, not the context.* IT may not understand how leaders need to use the tool in their work. Someone who uses Zoom for tech support by sharing a screen is going to use it very differently than those who are leading and communicating using the tools. Any training on a tool must be done in the context of how people will use it in real life.

- *Do they know?* Just because they're techies, doesn't mean they use the tool properly. We frequently notice that even though some IT people have used Teams for a long time, they aren't aware of some of the richer tools associated with it, like surveys and whiteboards. We aren't throwing anyone under the bus—they may never have needed to use those options. This observation just points out that they might not be the most qualified people to teach your leaders (or team members).

The Remote Team

This book is about leadership, and yet we can't talk about developing successful Long-Distance Leaders without acknowledging those on the team who work remotely and need support and additional skills. Teams only function at a high level when everyone has the same understanding of how to make things work in the real world. This is why we wrote *The Long-Distance Teammate*. You will find that text supports and expands on the ideas in this book with a focus on individual contributors.

Consider these questions:

- Do all team members understand the organization's mission and vision, goals and strategies, and how their work is aligned? (Remember, many of the cues and reminders that are available when people are working onsite are lost when they are working away from the office or plant.)

■ Do your individual team members know what is expected of them specifically related to working remotely?

■ If the work is hybrid, do they know what work is best accomplished in person and what should be done remotely or asynchronously?

■ Do they have the technical skills they need to get their work done?

■ Do they have the skills to communicate, build relationships, and trust successfully at a distance?

■ Do they know what is expected of them as a teammate, not just how to do their own work?

■ Do they have options for learning the skills they are missing?

And perhaps most important, how confident are you in your answers to all the questions in this chapter? If you are still reading, you are thinking about helping your Long-Distance Leaders succeed. Ultimately, they can't succeed without a successful team. Make sure you are supporting and developing them too.

Pause and Reflect

Note: In the rest of the book we have frequently urged you to pause and reflect. In this section, our focus is different. We aren't asking you to assess yourself or your team, rather, we're asking you to think at an organization level. This may involve conversations with people in other departments. We encourage those conversations and the actions they generate.

▶ What is the organizational culture we aspire to?

- ▶ How does remote or hybrid work impact that cultural vision?

- ▶ What behaviors should change to create that culture, especially for the remote team members?

- ▶ What behaviors and skills do I want my Long-Distance Leaders to exhibit?

- ▶ What gaps in skills and knowledge exist for my Long-Distance Leaders?

- ▶ What learning resources and materials do we have that correctly reflect the needs of the Long-Distance Leader?

- ▶ Which groups or parts of the organization should have a role in creating my leadership development plan (besides the training department)?

- ▶ How can I ensure these stakeholders are aligned so that the leadership development plans meet real world needs?

Online Resources

If you would like more help and ideas, go to KevinEikenberry.com for a complete list of our services, thought leadership, and free resources.

To identify the biggest skill and knowledge gaps in your organization directly related to working remotely, register at LongDistanceWorklife.com /Resources and request the Organizational Technology Assessment Tool.

You can access both of these sites with this QR code.

Epilogue

Before We Go

Rule 19: When all else fails, remember Rule 1.

Without continual growth and progress, such words as improvement, achievement, and success have no meaning.

—Benjamin Franklin, writer, scientist, inventor, statesman

This book is nearly complete, but we hope your work has just begun.

A book by itself is of little importance. We don't say that out of false modesty; only to put it into the proper context. If we have done our job, this book has done two, maybe three things:

- *It has educated you.* After all, you haven't been reading one of Wayne's novels (yes, he's written several—Google it). You picked up this book to learn something new about leading a team at a distance, to see something in a new way, or perhaps even to confirm that something you have been doing is "right," appropriate, and/or even a best practice.

- *It has inspired you.* Education without any inspiration is a dry exercise. Meaning no disrespect to any of your past teachers, we think you probably took some classes in school that may have educated you but didn't leave you very inspired. We hope you now have more hope, more confidence, and a sense of the value and importance of the acts of leadership, especially when distance makes leading even more complex.

- *It has entertained you.* While not as important (perhaps) as the first two things, we could argue that if you weren't entertained, the other two wouldn't have happened. After all, how many other books have you read that talk about the building of the pyramids, a football player in the 1960s, and Albanian klezmer music? The Kevin Eikenberry Group is partly based on the notion that learning can and should be fun.

But really, we have aspired to a fourth thing, the real purpose of this book.

- *It has led you to action.* Education, inspiration, and even entertainment are worthy goals, but they are only process goals. The *results* goal here is application; we hope that you go out and *do something* with what you learned. If you aren't more intentional about how you give feedback, if you don't learn to use your technology more effectively, if you don't help people reach the goals that are set, what was the point?

One of the best compliments Kevin received for his book *Remarkable Leadership* was "you can tell this book was written by a trainer. He is continually encouraging you to try what you are learning." Both of us are proud to wear the hat of trainer, teacher, and facilitator of learning. Both of us have spent many hours in a classroom (and on one side of a webcam) helping people from around the world learn new skills and approaches to leading and communicating more effectively. We wrote this book so you could do your work with more skill, effectiveness, and confidence.

But it is just a book.

Now the real (important) work begins.

If you are leaving these pages with tools and the confidence to go try them, we are pleased, proud, and honored.

And while the book may be ending, our commitment to helping those leading at a distance isn't.

At the close of many chapters, we have provided links to online resources. These assessments, checklists, and other tools were designed to give you more than the physical book allowed. They are available solely to those who have read the book. Please use them—that is why we created them.

Go to KevinEikenberry.com and see the scope of our products and services—there you'll find new ideas, new tools, our latest thinking on leadership, and other topics beyond the scope of this book. We are committed to helping leaders at a distance lead more effectively.

And while you are there, you can find links and phone numbers to contact us. Like all authors, we would love to hear from you, help you understand the questions we didn't answer (and hopefully give you some insight), hear how what we've written has made a difference, and in general, continue the conversation about being more effective as a Long-Distance Leader.

All the best to you, and with all due respect, get back to work leading at a distance more effectively.

Notes

Chapter 1

1. Jordan Turner, "9 Future of Work Trends for 2024," Gartner, January 3, 2024, https://www.gartner.com/en/articles/9-future-of-work-trends -for-2024.

Chapter 3

1. Karen Sobel Lojeski, *Leading the Virtual Workforce: How Great Leaders Transform Organizations in the 21st Century* (Hoboken, NJ: John Wiley and Sons, 2009).

Chapter 4

1. Based on *The CHAOS Report* (1994) by the Standish Group and revisited in 2007. Although there is considerable debate about the numbers, Jim Highsmith, in *Agile Project Management: Creating Innovative Products*, and other experts have concluded: "The Standish data are NOT a good indicator of poor software development performance. However, they ARE an indicator of systemic failure of our planning and measurement processes." He goes on to say that you can't use the Standish numbers to show return on investment, but they accurately predict end-user adoption and other cultural barriers to success.

2. Gerald C. Kane, Doug Palmer, Anh Nguyen Phillips, David Kiron, and Natasha Buckley, "Strategy, Not Technology Drives Digital Transformation: Becoming a Digitally Mature Enterprise," *MIT Sloan Management Review*, July 14, 2015, https://sloanreview.mit.edu/projects/strategy-drives -digital-transformation/, and Michael Fitzgerald, Nina Kruschwitz, Didier

Bonnet, and Michael Welch, "Embracing Digital Technology: A New Strategic Imperative," *MIT Sloan Management Review*, October 7, 2013, https://sloanreview.mit.edu/projects/embracing-digital-technology/.

Chapter 5

1. For more on servant leadership, see the Robert K. Greenleaf Center for Servant Leadership, https://www.greenleaf.org/what-is-servant-leadership.
2. Ovidijus Jurevicius, "Mission Statement of McDonald's," Strategic Management Insight, September 14, 2013, https://www.strategicmanagementinsight.com/mission-statements/mcdonalds-mission-statement.html.
3. Barbara Farfan, "Google Business Profile and Mission Statement," The Balance, July 13, 2017, https://www.thebalance.com/google-business-profile-2892814.
4. Justin Kruger and David Dunning, "Unskilled and Unaware of It: How Difficulties in Recognizing One's Own Incompetence Lead to Inflated Self-Assessments," *Journal of Personality and Social Psychology* 77, no. 6 (1999): 1121–34.

Chapter 8

1. Marshall Goldsmith, Laurence S. Lyons, and Sarah McArthur, *Coaching for Leadership: Writings on Leadership from the World's Greatest Coaches*, 3rd ed. (San Francisco: Pfeiffer, 2012).
2. Thomas J. Peters, Robert H. Waterman, *In Search of Excellence: Lessons from America's Best-Run Companies* (New York: HarperCollins, 1982/2006).

Chapter 10

1. Hilary Silver, "Working from Home: Before and After the Pandemic," *Journal of the American Sociological Association* 22, no.1 (Winter 2023): 66–70.

Chapter 11

1. James M. Kouzes, Barry Z. Posner, *The Leadership Challenge: How to Make Extraordinary Things Happen in Organizations*, 6th ed. (Hoboken, NJ: John Wiley and Sons, 2017).

2. Elise Keith, "How Many Meetings Are There per Day in 2022?," Lucid Meetings, accessed March 19, 2024, https://blog.lucidmeetings.com/blog/how-many-meetings-are-there-per-day-in-2022/.

Chapter 12

1. Bettina S. T. Büchel, *Using Communication Technology* (New York: Palgrave, 2001).

Chapter 13

1. Gerald C. Kane, Doug Palmer, Anh Nguyen Phillips, David Kiron, and Natasha Buckley, "Strategy, Not Technology Drives Digital Transformation," *MIT Sloan Management Review* (July 14, 2015), https://sloanreview.mit.edu/projects/strategy-drives-digital-transformation/, and Michael Fitzgerald, Nina Kruschwitz, Didier Bonnet, and Michael Welch, "Embracing Digital Technology: A New Strategic Imperative," *MIT Sloan Management Review* (October 7, 2013), https://sloanreview.mit.edu/projects/embracing-digital-technology

2. Jared Spataro, "Remote Work Trend Report: Meetings," *Microsoft 365* (blog), April 9, 2020, https://www.microsoft.com/en-us/microsoft-365/blog/2020/04/09/remote-work-trend-report-meetings.

3. "True Wireless Confessions: How People Really Use Mobile Devices," Verizon, June 30, 2015, https://www.verizon.com/about/news/vzw/2015/06/how-people-really-use-their-mobile-devices.

Chapter 15

1. Pauline Rose Clance and Suzanne Imes, "The Imposter Phenomenon in High Achieving Women: Dynamics and Therapeutic Intervention," *Psychotherapy Theory, Research and Practice* 15, no. 3 (1978), http://www.paulineroseclance.com/pdf/ip_high_achieving_women.pdf.

Recommended Reading

Bell, Chip R., and Marshall Goldsmith. *Managers as Mentors: Building Partner-ships for Learning.* Oakland, CA: Berrett-Koehler Publishers, 2013.

Booher, Dianna. *Communicate Like a Leader: Connecting Strategically to Coach, Inspire, and Get Things Done.* Oakland, CA: Berrett-Koehler Publishers, 2017.

Büchel, Bettina S. *Using Communication Technology: Creating Knowledge Orga-nizations.* New York: Palgrave MacMillan, 2001.

Burkus, David. *Leading From Anywhere: The Essential Guide to Managing Remote Teams.* Boston: Mariner Books, 2021

Covey, Stephen M. R. *The Speed of Trust: The One Thing That Changes Every-thing.* New York: Free Press, 2008.

Drucker, Peter F. *The Effective Executive: The Definitive Guide to Getting the Right Things Done.* New York: HarperCollins, 2006.

Dyer, Chris. *Remote Work: Redesign Processes, Practices and Strategies to Engage a Remote Workforce.* New York: Kogan Page, 2021.

Eikenberry, Kevin. *Remarkable Leadership: Unleashing Your Leadership Poten-tial One Skill at a Time.* San Francisco: Jossey-Bass, 2007.

Eikenberry, Kevin, and Guy Harris. *From Bud to Boss: Secrets to a Successful Transition to Remarkable Leadership.* San Francisco: Jossey-Bass, 2011.

Gentry, William. *Be the Boss Everyone Wants to Work For: A Guide for New Leaders.* Oakland, CA: Berrett-Koehler Publishers, 2016.

Greene, Ali, and Tamara Sanderson. *Remote Works: Managing for Freedom, Flexibility, and Focus.* Oakland, CA: Berrett-Koehler, 2023.

Kahnweiler, Jennifer B. *The Genius of Opposites: How Introverts and Extroverts Achieve Extraordinary Results Together.* Oakland, CA: Berrett-Koehler Pub-lishers, 2015.

Kouzes, James M., and Barry Z. Posner. *The Leadership Challenge: How to Make Extraordinary Things Happen in Organizations*, 6th ed. Hoboken, NJ: John Wiley and Sons, 2017.

Maxwell, John C. *The 21 Irrefutable Laws of Leadership: Follow Them and People Will Follow You*. Nashville, TN: Thomas Nelson, 2007.

Rad, Parvis F., and Ginger Levin. *Achieving Project Management Success Using Virtual Teams*. Boca Raton, FL: J. Ross Publishing, 2003.

Sayers, Gale, and Al Silverman. *I Am Third: The Inspiration for Brian's Song*, 3rd ed. New York: Penguin Books, 2001.

Stanier, Michael Bungay. *The Coaching Habit: Say Less, Ask More and Change the Way You Lead Forever*. Toronto, ON: Box of Crayons Press, 2016.

Turmel, Wayne. *Meet Like You Mean It: A Leader's Guide to Painless and Productive Virtual Meetings*. Lisle, IL: Achis Marketing Services, 2014.

Zofi, Yael. *A Manager's Guide to Virtual Teams*. New York: AMACOM, 2012.

Acknowledgments

A book like this requires the help of a lot of people and, fittingly, they are scattered far and wide.

First, there's the team we work with every day at The Kevin Eikenberry Group and the Remote Leadership Institute. From Richmond to Phoenix, Chicago to Indianapolis, you continue to amaze us with your hard work, keen insight, and cheerful support. In particular, thanks to Erica Brown for her assisting with the graphics and helping us put our words into pictures.

We're grateful to the team at Berrett-Koehler for their faith in us, as well as for their early support and for and keeping us focused on this project and on a constantly changing target. Specifically, Neal Maillet and Jeevan Sivasubramaniam as well as the production team, and everyone involved in marketing and promotion also deserve a nod. Without them, you likely wouldn't be reading this. Roger Peterson helped us polish our ideas and create a better first edition of this book. Rebecca Rider has helped us make this better with her astute questions and excellent editing.

Finally, to our valued customers: it's our pleasure to serve, work with, and learn from you. It's our sincere hope that this book makes your journey a little less arduous.

Beyond this, here are some personal thoughts from each of us.

From Kevin . . .

Beyond our overall acknowledgment of the team, I must say more. I believe this book is better because I have the chance to lead this remote team each day. Many of the ideas have been tested and honed through my interactions with our team. What I have learned from them can't be overstated. Finally, I thank my wife, Lori, for her patience, understanding, and support—not just while writing this book but throughout our lives. She makes me better every day in every way.

From Wayne...

People have been writing leadership books since the *Code of Hammurabi*, and we merely stand on their shoulders. It would be both rude to ignore and impossible to count them all, but this hopefully adds to the collective wisdom. Also, I must acknowledge my wife, Joan (the Duchess), for all of her unstinting support and incredible patience.

Index

About the Authors

Kevin Eikenberry

Kevin Eikenberry is a recognized world expert on leadership development and learning and the Chief Potential Officer of The Kevin Eikenberry Group.

Kevin has spent more than thirty years helping organizations across North America and leaders from around the world with leadership, learning, teams and teamwork, communication, and more. His client list includes Fortune 500 companies, small firms, universities, government agencies, and hospitals. Past clients include names you'll recognize: the American Red Cross, Chevron Phillips Chemical Company, Cirque du Soleil, John Deere, LG Electronics, Purdue University, Southwest Airlines, and many more.

He is the author of the bestselling books *Remarkable Leadership* and *Vantagepoints on Learning and Life*. He coauthored with Guy Harris another bestseller, *From Bud to Boss: Secrets of the Successful Transition to Remarkable Leadership*, and a companion book titled *My Journey from Bud to Boss*. He has also written two other books with Wayne—*The Long-Distance Teammate* and *The Long-Distance Team*. Beyond these, he is a contributing author to more than fifteen other books.

Kevin has created eLearning materials on many of the most prominent platforms used around the world, including LinkedIn Learning. At last count his books and learning materials have been translated into thirteen languages.

He has been named as one of the top one hundred leadership and management thinkers in the world by Inc.com and among the Top 30 Leadership Professionals by Global Gurus.com three years running.

Wayne Turmel

Wayne Turmel is a cofounder of the Remote Leadership Institute. He has spent the last twenty-five years or more obsessed by how people communicate at work. His work has helped organizations on four continents develop the communication skills needed to lead people, projects, and teams and to make the adjustment to remote working and virtual teams.

Wayne is the author of several books, including ATD's *10 Steps to Successful Virtual Presentations* and *Meet Like You Mean It: A Leader's Guide to Painless and Productive Virtual Meetings*. He's also contributed to almost a dozen other books, and his groundbreaking podcasts *The Long-Distance Worklife* and *The Cranky Middle Manager Show* have been entertaining and informing audiences for years. His clients have included the American Red Cross, Schneider Electric, Dell, and several departments of the US and Canadian governments.

Marshall Goldsmith has called Wayne "one of the truly unique voices in leadership."

About Our Services

Helping Your Leaders and Teams—
Whether at a Distance or Together!

You and your leaders are leading, and not just remotely!

This book has helped you think about the challenges and opportunities of leading at a distance, but you likely have other challenges, needs, and questions.

The Kevin Eikenberry Group has been helping leaders become more effective, confident, and successful since 1993.

And now we'd like to help you.

We offer a variety of learning, coaching, and consulting services to help leaders and organizations succeed. Along with our expertise for all things Long-Distance work, we have extensive experience in working with teams, new and frontline leaders, and leaders of leaders—regardless of where they work.

We know this book is just the tip of the iceberg in your leadership journey. Here are just a few of the other ways we can work together.

More learning opportunities. We offer a variety of learning opportunities, from live learning events and workshops—both in-person and virtually delivered—to trainer certification, to on-demand offerings and eLearning tools that provide targeted and just-in-time learning.

More help. If you are looking for tailored learning options inside your organization, coaching for one or more leaders, or guidance with broader organizational needs, we can help.

More tools. We offer a variety of free online resources to help you and your organization succeed. Our blog shares lessons from clients and our latest thinking on leadership, organizational development, and the continually evolving picture of the remote working world. Explore our website for this and our collection of learning tools and resources.

- All resources from this book as well as information about the other books in the Long-Distance Worklife series (and the Long-Distance Worklife podcast) can be found at LongDistanceWorklife.com.

- Our products and services, blog and much more can be found at KevinEikenberry.com.

- Sign up for our free newsletters at KevinEikenberry.com/newsletters.

- Sign up for our unique video series, *13 Days to Remarkable Leadership,* at KevinEikenberry.com/13Days.

- Connect with Wayne and Kevin on LinkedIn for regular content and to let us know how else we can assist you and your organization.

  Use this QR code for easy access to all of these links.

Berrett–Koehler
Publishers

Berrett-Koehler is an independent publisher dedicated to an ambitious mission: *Connecting people and ideas to create a world that works for all.*

Our publications span many formats, including print, digital, audio, and video. We also offer online resources, training, and gatherings. And we will continue expanding our products and services to advance our mission.

We believe that the solutions to the world's problems will come from all of us, working at all levels: in our society, in our organizations, and in our own lives. Our publications and resources offer pathways to creating a more just, equitable, and sustainable society. They help people make their organizations more humane, democratic, diverse, and effective (and we don't think there's any contradiction there). And they guide people in creating positive change in their own lives and aligning their personal practices with their aspirations for a better world.

And we strive to practice what we preach through what we call "The BK Way." At the core of this approach is *stewardship,* a deep sense of responsibility to administer the company for the benefit of all of our stakeholder groups, including authors, customers, employees, investors, service providers, sales partners, and the communities and environment around us. Everything we do is built around stewardship and our other core values of *quality, partnership, inclusion,* and *sustainability.*

This is why Berrett-Koehler is the first book publishing company to be both a B Corporation (a rigorous certification) and a benefit corporation (a for-profit legal status), which together require us to adhere to the highest standards for corporate, social, and environmental performance. And it is why we have instituted many pioneering practices (which you can learn about at www.bkconnection.com), including the Berrett-Koehler Constitution, the Bill of Rights and Responsibilities for BK Authors, and our unique Author Days.

We are grateful to our readers, authors, and other friends who are supporting our mission. We ask you to share with us examples of how BK publications and resources are making a difference in your lives, organizations, and communities at www.bkconnection.com/impact.

Dear reader,

Thank you for picking up this book and welcome to the worldwide BK community! You're joining a special group of people who have come together to create positive change in their lives, organizations, and communities.

What's BK all about?

Our mission is to connect people and ideas to create a world that works for all.

Why? Our communities, organizations, and lives get bogged down by old paradigms of self-interest, exclusion, hierarchy, and privilege. But we believe that can change. That's why we seek the leading experts on these challenges—and share their actionable ideas with you.

A welcome gift

To help you get started, we'd like to offer you a **free copy** of one of our bestselling ebooks:

www.bkconnection.com/welcome

When you claim your **free ebook**, you'll also be subscribed to our blog.

Our freshest insights

Access the best new tools and ideas for leaders at all levels on our blog at ideas.bkconnection.com.

Sincerely,

Your friends at Berrett-Koehler

Berrett–Koehler
Publishers

Berrett-Koehler is an independent publisher dedicated to an ambitious mission: *Connecting people and ideas to create a world that works for all.*

Our publications span many formats, including print, digital, audio, and video. We also offer online resources, training, and gatherings. And we will continue expanding our products and services to advance our mission.

We believe that the solutions to the world's problems will come from all of us, working at all levels: in our society, in our organizations, and in our own lives. Our publications and resources offer pathways to creating a more just, equitable, and sustainable society. They help people make their organizations more humane, democratic, diverse, and effective (and we don't think there's any contradiction there). And they guide people in creating positive change in their own lives and aligning their personal practices with their aspirations for a better world.

And we strive to practice what we preach through what we call "The BK Way." At the core of this approach is *stewardship,* a deep sense of responsibility to administer the company for the benefit of all of our stakeholder groups, including authors, customers, employees, investors, service providers, sales partners, and the communities and environment around us. Everything we do is built around stewardship and our other core values of *quality, partnership, inclusion,* and *sustainability.*

This is why Berrett-Koehler is the first book publishing company to be both a B Corporation (a rigorous certification) and a benefit corporation (a for-profit legal status), which together require us to adhere to the highest standards for corporate, social, and environmental performance. And it is why we have instituted many pioneering practices (which you can learn about at www.bkconnection.com), including the Berrett-Koehler Constitution, the Bill of Rights and Responsibilities for BK Authors, and our unique Author Days.

We are grateful to our readers, authors, and other friends who are supporting our mission. We ask you to share with us examples of how BK publications and resources are making a difference in your lives, organizations, and communities at www.bkconnection.com/impact.

Dear reader,

Thank you for picking up this book and welcome to the worldwide BK community! You're joining a special group of people who have come together to create positive change in their lives, organizations, and communities.

What's BK all about?

Our mission is to connect people and ideas to create a world that works for all.

Why? Our communities, organizations, and lives get bogged down by old paradigms of self-interest, exclusion, hierarchy, and privilege. But we believe that can change. That's why we seek the leading experts on these challenges—and share their actionable ideas with you.

A welcome gift

To help you get started, we'd like to offer you a **free copy** of one of our bestselling ebooks:

www.bkconnection.com/welcome

When you claim your **free ebook**, you'll also be subscribed to our blog.

Our freshest insights

Access the best new tools and ideas for leaders at all levels on our blog at ideas.bkconnection.com.

Sincerely,

Your friends at Berrett-Koehler